I'll GET BACK TO YOU

The Dyscommunication Crisis:
Why Unreturned Messages
Drive Us Crazy
and What to Do About It

SAM GEORGE

Post Hill
PRESS

A POST HILL PRESS BOOK
ISBN: 978-1-64293-719-0
ISBN (eBook): 978-1-64293-720-6

I'll Get Back to You:
The Dyscommunication Crisis: Why Unreturned Messages
Drive Us Crazy and What to Do About It

Cover art by Ken Aronson

Post Hill Press
New York • Nashville
posthillpress.com

Published in the United States of America
1 2 3 4 5 6 7 8 9 10

To my grandfather, Martin Shanahan,
who taught me how to think.

A very special thanks to Dr. Robert Williams who recently passed away due to COVID. He is the founder of the Biological Psychiatry Institute. His understanding of the mind's patterns and what happens when these patterns are broken is essential to the book.

CONTENTS

The darkness, the loop of negative thoughts on repeat,
clamors and interferes with the music I hear in my head.
—Lady Gaga

INTRODUCTION

The Threat That's Hiding in Plain Sight

It was, potentially, the end of the world as we knew it. For thirteen days, the world held its collective breath as two superpowers stood on the brink of nuclear war. One could argue that the world was suspended in a deathly limbo due to nothing more than unreturned messages, or more accurately, the precursor to our modern text messages: wire telegrams.

It all began on October 14, 1962, when a U.S. U-2 spy plane flew over the Cuban countryside and discovered that Cuba, the U.S.'s neighbor to the south, indeed had Soviet long-range nuclear weapons, powerful enough to reach Mexico City, Seattle, L.A., and New York City, and enough in quantity to hit every major U.S. city in between as well.

The threat to all of humanity was hiding in plain sight.

Back in Washington, D.C., President John F. Kennedy assembled a team of advisors, called ExComm. For several days they discussed their options. If war commenced between two nuclear powers—Soviet-backed Cuba and the U.S.—it wouldn't just mean millions of U.S. and Cuban citizens' lives lost: it could mean the end of human existence on planet Earth. The stakes weren't just high, they were permanent. The fate of humanity rested in two mighty, yet headstrong leaders' ability to communicate: the President of the United States and the Chairman of the Soviet Union, Nikita Khrushchev.

October 22, after several days of weighing his options and discussing them with the ExComm team, Kennedy finally called on U.S. ambassador to the Soviet Union, Foy Kohler, to deliver a message via encrypted telegram to Khrushchev, asking him to remove the missiles. He added, "I have not assumed that you or any other sane man would, in this nuclear age, deliberately plunge the world into war which it is crystal clear no country could win and which could only result in catastrophic consequences to the whole world, including the aggressor."[1]

For hours, Kennedy waited. And waited. And then waited some more. Meanwhile, the ExComm scrambled trying to figure out what to do and ran through all the worst-case scenarios. The worst, of course, being the complete annihilation of humanity.

Can you imagine what Kennedy was thinking as he waited for Khrushchev to reply? *Does the lag in time mean that the Soviets are preparing for an all-out assault? What about my wife, Caroline, and Jack? Do I need to get them out of Washington, D.C.? What if they strike here first? What about all the U.S. citizens? What happens if I wait? Could he be preparing a launch at this moment?*

Of course, we can only imagine what was going on in Kennedy's mind during this wait time. And because he had no idea what Khrushchev was thinking, he had to anticipate his next move, make assumptions about the man's thinking and motives, and, like most of us waiting for a message to be returned, try to quash his anxiety so he could think clearly and strategize. *Will Khrushchev preemptively strike? Will he see the quarantine that Kennedy and ExComm have instituted as an act of war? What should the U.S. do? Should the U.S. strike first? Does Khrushchev think I am weak? That I don't have it in me to take him down?*

On October 23, a full day after Kennedy has sent the encrypted telegram, Khrushchev writes back to the president and rebuffs Kennedy's demands to remove the missiles, arguing they are "intended solely for defensive purposes."[2] On the same day, Kennedy writes back, in what can only feel like, in today's lingo, "a text battle" for the ages. Kennedy risks everything—all of humanity's lives, in fact—with a literal puerile "you started it" argument, bluntly reminding Khrushchev he "started the crisis by secretly sending missiles to Cuba."[3] Things escalate quickly from there. Can you imagine what Khrushchev is thinking? *Who does this guy think he is? Sending me a message like that?*

For twenty-four hours, Kennedy doesn't hear a thing. He can only imagine and begin to think of worst-case scenarios— that Khrushchev is obviously using this time to plan an offensive attack. Kennedy's team reacts. U.S. ambassador Adlai Stevenson explains the matter to the U.N. Security Council and dispatches U.S. ships to the Caribbean. At the same time, Soviet submarines move toward it as well. While the gap in communication grows, war vessels proceed toward each other, closing a gap of their own.

Finally, on October 24, Khrushchev sends yet another indignant message to Kennedy, stating "You're no longer appealing to reason, but wish to intimidate us."[4]

Things escalate quickly from here. The U.S. raises for the first time ever its nuclear war alert to the highest level—DEFCON 2. This is just one step below DEFCON 1, which means the nuclear threat is immediately imminent. U.S. nuclear-armed missiles are placed on alert. All it would take is one misunderstanding, one misinterpreted or ambiguous message, one false assumption, and a full-blown nuclear exchange would likely ensue. Participants close to the president and part of the ExComm team believe they'll never see their loved ones again and begin to make arrangements.

On October 26, Premier Fidel Castro also writes to Khrushchev. Instead of asking him to stand down, he begs his ally to launch a nuclear strike and attack the U.S. Khrushchev is waiting now to see what the U.S. will do. *Will they launch missiles from nearby Turkey and take out Moscow in retaliation? What about his own people? He can't abide being shown up by the young president in the U.S. He must show the world who is boss. One of them is going to act,* Khrushchev thinks, *so why not be the first to do so?* After all, Khrushchev has no idea what Kennedy is thinking. The delays in communication only add to the assumptions.

Then on October 27, another U.S. U-2 spy plane, piloted by Major Rudolf Anderson, flies over Cuba and is immediately shot down. Major Anderson is killed. Nuclear attack is now most certainly imminent. The perception is that Soviet-Cuba forces fired the first shot, and the U.S. can go ahead and strike back at will.

The world watches. It can do nothing but wait. And, of course, fear the worst.

Obviously, writing the equivalent of heated text messages between two foreign powers is not proving to be the best way to avoid nuclear annihilation. That same evening, Kennedy decides he's had enough with the delayed responses and electronic messages. It's time to have a good old-fashioned face-to-face meeting. He sends his brother, Attorney General Robert Kennedy, to meet with the Soviet ambassador Anatoly Dobrynin. In what is now a declassified telegram, Dobrynin recounted his face-to-face meeting with Robert Kennedy, and explained to Khrushchev, in plain and clear language, that the U.S. did not want to fire in response, quoting Kennedy, who said "a chain reaction will quickly start that will be very hard to stop...a real war will begin, in which millions of Americans and Russians will die. We want to avoid that any way we can, I'm sure that the government of the USSR has the same wish."[5] The ambassador also relays to Khrushchev that during the course of their discussion, Kennedy admits that his brother, the president, is willing to negotiate removing missiles in Turkey in exchange for the Soviet removal of their missiles in Cuba if it means avoiding nuclear catastrophe. This of course is all "Top Secret," and Kennedy doesn't want the information leaked because it would affect the U.S.'s standing with NATO. By the end of Dobrynin's telegram to Khrushchev, he explains that the U.S. has no intention of starting a nuclear war with the Soviets.

The face-to-face meeting between the attorney general and the Soviet ambassador and the subsequent communication between the ambassador and Khrushchev ultimately led to Khrushchev conceding and agreeing publicly to the removal of missiles—and of course, the avoiding of a nuclear holocaust. Thus, the private meeting made it possible for negotiation and the revelation of top-secret intel that couldn't be shared otherwise.

As soon as Khrushchev announced publicly that they are removing the missiles, Kennedy—and the world—exhaled.

A year later, Kennedy and Khrushchev do something incredible, truly telling of what was the crux of the crisis that almost annihilated human existence: communication.

On August 30, 1963, both Kennedy and Khrushchev have special phones installed in their offices, which served as a direct phone line between the White House and the Kremlin in Moscow. The "hotline" was intended to facilitate convenient communication between the two countries. In the wake of what is now known as the Cuban Missile Crisis, both Kennedy and Khrushchev realized "that the highly tense diplomatic exchange that followed was plagued by delays caused by slow and tedious communication systems."[6] Although Kennedy and Khrushchev were able to resolve the crisis without incident, they nevertheless underestimated what they called "fears" of future Dyscommunication, so they installed an improved communications system, which would allow for swift responses and remove any risk of either country jumping to inaccurate conclusions or, as the White House-issued statement said, "help reduce the risk of war occurring by accident or miscalculation."[7]

Imagine setting off World War III *by accident*? Because you catastrophized and preemptively acted while waiting for a delayed or unreturned message? Granted, in the case of Khrushchev and Kennedy, their "worst-case" scenario thinking was indeed the definitive worst case. They weren't being melodramatic when they were saying the fate of humanity was in their hands. But it is, nevertheless, the most profound example of how devastating delayed communications can be while thinking the worst about message senders and recipients.

Thankfully, neither man acted out his worst impulses. Together they used this dangerous crisis as an opportunity to improve communication. Now instead of relying on telegrammed letters that had to travel overseas, this "new technology" meant American and Soviet leaders could simply pick up the phone and be instantly connected twenty-four hours a day, seven days a week. No one would be waiting, wondering, catastrophizing, agonizing, or acting preemptively and making matters worse. And, for that matter, blowing up the world.

Ironically, the one thing that was considered lifesaving and crucial to solving the crisis—face-to-face and/or direct communication—has gone the way of the Soviet Union itself and is virtually obsolete now. In our current day and age, we have drastically reduced not only face-to-face meetings but telephone calls as well. Instead, we rely primarily on text and email communications, and to our own peril. This shift from face-to-face or real-time communications via the telephone has resulted in a paradigm shift. In other words, the construct of the way we communicate has created a crisis hiding in plain sight. Just like the Cuban missiles and their threat to humanity went undetected until the U-2 spy planes spotted them, we have been unaware what a serious threat to our humanity this crisis in communication means for all of us—until now.

Though most of us who don't return a phone call or find ourselves waiting for a return don't have the fate of the world hanging in our hands, it often feels like it does in the moment. So many of us have found ourselves in similar situations as Kennedy was during those crucial seven days of the thirteen-day ordeal, waiting for a response and left to wonder what the other guy is thinking, or worse, what they are about to do. Left in the dark with our own thoughts, we can spin out, think the worst, grow agitated, become fearful, believe the lack of response has something to do with us, and then act in ways we may regret later.

What seemed like an easy answer to resolving this communication problem—installing phones in order to reply right away—even as late as the sixties, isn't so easy now. Remarkably, with more ways to communicate than ever, we humans have found more ways to misinterpret each other and jump to conclusions. We now have texts, emails, DMs—hundreds of them—coming at us each day. It is easy to forget to respond to someone or leave them hanging. It's also incredibly common to feel like the world is coming to an end when someone hasn't texted or emailed us back.

A Crisis of Our Own: Why Dyscommunication Isn't Just a Misunderstanding

The crisis we are facing is caused by delayed and ambiguous communication. However, the series of responses to the crisis, such as taking it personally, jumping to worst-case scenarios, catastrophizing, and possibly doing something we regret, are what I refer to as the Dyscommunication Syndrome. The Dycommunication Syndrome goes beyond misunderstanding into the realm of dysfunction—hence the term Dyscommunication.

And I call it a syndrome, not because it is classified as a diagnosable psychiatric medical condition one can look up in the American Psychiatric Association's DSM, but because like all medical syndromes, Dyscommunication Syndrome presents itself as a set of symptoms correlated with each other and associated with one particular occurrence. In fact, the word *syndrome* derives from a Greek word meaning *concurrence*. Everyone who experiences it experiences a *concurrence* of symptoms in a similar way. So for the purposes of this book, instead of repeatedly listing the concurrence of symptoms (which I classify into seven parts: anxiety and agitation, taking it personally, resentment and distrust, catastrophizing, thinking about (or even doing) something you'll regret, an inability to talk yourself down, and feeling ashamed), I'll refer to them collectively as Dyscommunication Syndrome or DCS. It's time we give this pervasive genre of angst a name so that we can learn how to avoid it.

So why call it Dyscommunication Syndrome? It was common for centuries in the medical community to name syndromes after scientists and physicians who discovered or made the connection between the syndromes, for example Wolf-Hirschhorn or Anderson Disorders were named after their founders, or the first people to describe them. However, I don't particularly want the name of a syndrome linked to anxiety and catastrophizing to be named the Sam George Syndrome. (However, if there is a syndrome or a gene linked to happiness and positivity, I'll gladly take it!) In the meantime, I'll stick with the more modern approach, which is to name conditions descriptively by the symptoms or underlying causes.

But then why not name the condition Miscommunication Syndrome? Simply put, miscommunication is when a message that has been *sent* is misunderstood. Dyscommunication is when a message is neither understood nor misunderstood because the message is unreturned, delayed, or answered ambiguously. We are left in limbo, and our minds start churning to fill in the blanks and close the broken loop. As in the case of the Cuban Missile Crisis—it wasn't what was being said that was the cause of the crisis, it was the delay. The gap in between the communication became fertile ground for the leaders' minds to begin to make assumptions, take things personally, act irrationally, and even act in a way that they would ultimately regret.

To clarify: *Dyscommunication is a break in the feedback loop of communication.* Unlike communication in person or by phone, there is no immediate feedback loop. With digital communication, there is a gap between a message and its response. And this gap occurs when the way we communicate is via digital means—specifically text messages and emails. But of course, there are many, many digital means these days as well, but for the purposes of this book, I'll focus on texts and emails.

▌ Today's Crisis Hiding in Plain Sight

On a Tuesday morning at 6:45, the alarm on Mary's smartphone chimes. She groggily reaches over to turn the alarm off and can't help but check her email. While she's reading the chain of emails from her boss, each containing a separate question about a project that's due on Friday, Mary gets the first text of the day—the neighbor's child needs to go to urgent care, could she send her daughter over to Mary's before school this morning? In her haze, Mary responds "sure" and starts answering the boss's questions, one by one. By the time she's finished, she's already running behind. So, she rouses the kids and hops in the shower, which is why she missed the text from her neighbor that says, "Sending her over! Text when she gets there?"

Mary doesn't hear the doorbell ring when her neighbor's daughter arrives—she'd forgotten all about that text exchange—and the girl has to wait on the porch for fifteen minutes while Mary dries off and gets dressed (the kids are slow to rise and her husband's already left for work). When she grabs her phone to walk downstairs, she sees the text she missed from her neighbor, as well as the multiple "Everything OK? She should be there" texts that followed. She lets the girl in, hollers up at the kids to get dressed, and texts her neighbor back. She's already received five texts and answered five emails before she's even had a cup of coffee. And that's just the beginning of the communications Mary will send and receive that day.

According to technology consulting firm Radicati, the average American sends and receives 72 texts and receives 126 emails per day. Aside from sheer quantity, every one of those interactions brings with it an invitation for Dyscommunication. Your call doesn't get returned. The email doesn't really answer your question, making you fear you've been misconstrued. The text is riddled with so many misspellings or bad guesses by the autocorrect feature that you aren't quite sure what it means. You are left to fill in the blanks on your own, and the stories you concoct about *why* your boss isn't writing you back, or *why* your friend texted you gobbledygook, or *why* your child's teacher didn't answer your question aren't pretty...maybe they are mad at you? Maybe you did something wrong that you didn't realize you did? Or maybe they have been killed in a tragic accident? It doesn't take long for our minds to start envisioning worst-case scenarios.

Why We Do This

Why do we do this to ourselves? Why do we keep returning to the same pattern of negative thoughts again and again? Why do we go immediately to the worst-case scenario? Why do we exacerbate drama, sometimes to the point of losing productivity and sleep? And why do we beat ourselves up when we discover that the reason our message went unreturned had nothing to do with us (because it very, very rarely has anything to do with us)?

It's straightforward: The human mind seeks closure. Our brain *hates* open loops, or what I call broken loops. After all, the brain is essentially a highly evolved pattern recognition machine, and an open loop is an incomplete pattern, hence a broken loop. In Ray Kurzweil's groundbreaking book, *How to Create a Mind: The Secret of Human Thought Revealed,* he takes apart the human brain and explains in rich detail how our brains are similar to machines (computers) that store information in patterns through a process he calls sequential ordering. This, he argues, allows for extraordinary progressions to take place. We need not remember an entire sequence for our mind to recall or retrieve information. All we need is a small hint. Have you ever smelled garlic roasting in an oven and suddenly been transported back to your grandmother's kitchen when you were five years old? Or have you ever listened to a song on the radio and immediately began thinking of an ex, and then have perfect recall of an outfit they were wearing or where you were both headed when you heard the song together? You may also begin to feel associated emotions related to that person, your breakup, or even grieving the loss of the relationship as well. You may even begin to wonder where they are, what they are doing, and if they think of you. Once your mind opens the floodgates, it will be hard to stop thinking the thoughts, and soon emotions will follow.

According to Kurzweil, our brains get tipped off and begin filling the blanks quite quickly; this is all thanks to our modern sapient part of the brain, the neocortex, which I'll refer to as the advanced mind or thinking brain throughout the course of this book. While our instinctive brain, or what is commonly referred to as our reptilian (old) brain, relies on the amygdala to interpret sensations (such as touching something hot and knowing instinctively to remove your hand), it's the neocortex, or advanced mind, that processes the information in a meaningful way. The sensory information from the amygdala is fed back to the neocortex where the spindle cells do their magic and remember, or store, the pattern, helping to create a strong emotional response to help you remember not to do that again. In fact, all our strong responses—love, anger, despair, joy, desire—are stored in this way. Have you ever had someone cut you off in traffic and cause you to nearly crash? Have you felt the rage rise in your body and find yourself shouting at the offender? Then months later, a car nearly swerves in your lane but backs out at the last minute. Nevertheless, though you realize you were in no real danger, your mind immediately goes to white hot rage all over again. That's pattern recognition. Your mind completed the story that you were in danger, and your body and emotions responded in kind. Have you ever not heard back from someone and immediately responded in anger or anxiety? This too is your brain going into overdrive after a triggering event. Usually, it can't stop until there seems to be a sense of closure. What is the best way to get closure? For most of us it's to complete the story with a worst-case scenario verdict. There is nothing more final or complete than saying something like "my friend hates me and is never going to talk to me again," or "my daughter is probably dead in a ditch somewhere because she hasn't texted me back in over an hour," or "of course the world is going to end from a nuclear holocaust." Our brains hate broken loops or open-ended thinking. Best to just end it, even if the "end" is indeed as final an ending as there is—like complete abandonment or death.

So why the worst-case scenario? Because our brain will go to great lengths to fill in the blanks of any communication that isn't resolved, and the result is a lot of emotional upset. Why? Because we are basically wired to look for closure. Invariably, we will create drama where there is none simply to satisfy our brain's need to complete a pattern.

The Two Main Factors Contributing to Our Collective Crazy

Like in the Cuban Missile Crisis, there are two things at work during this modern crisis of communication we face: 1) Our brain's tendency toward spiral-thinking and catastrophizing thanks to broken loops—or Dyscommunication Syndrome (DCS), and 2) the current communication construct we're forced to operate in, namely digital communications, creates a gap between the sender and receiver. The former determines how we respond, and the latter how we are now forced to communicate our response. For example, thirty years ago when the telephone rang, we answered it. We were asked a question and could give a response immediately. Only three ways could we send and receive messages: in person, via a letter in the mail or telegram, or through the telephone. It is the direct communication of face-to-face and telephone conversations that our minds need to complete a pattern or broken loop. But then came digital messages by way of emails and texts. Though the modes of communication have changed, our brains haven't. Our minds want to treat emails and texts as phone conversations as well. The modern mind craves immediate responses. And when that doesn't happen? Broken loops. Text exchanges mimic conversations just as if you were talking to someone over the phone or even in person. However, unlike those telephone or in-person communications, one of the parties can suddenly stop mid-sentence. When someone stops texting you in the middle of your "conversation," it feels like the equivalent of someone getting up from a chair and walking away from you mid-conversation with no explanation. Imagine having coffee with a friend and they suddenly stand up and walk out of the coffee shop? Wouldn't it be infuriating? Confusing? And it would feel completely out of the blue, right? Wouldn't your mind begin to wonder: *What the hell is happening? Is it something I said? Did something terrible happen?* Similarly, your brain doesn't know the difference amid a conversation via text or email. In fact, Gmail refers to email exchanges as "conversations" and bundles the emails together to emulate a conversation. Mail is not even used very often these days anymore, and it's not used as a means of conversation. Rather, it is a correspondence. The expectation is that of course there will be a delay. No one who wants an immediate answer would even think of sending a letter to get an immediate response. Instead they opt for emails or texts. Emails, texts, DMs, Facebook messages, and cloud-based work sharing sites are all now means to send and receive communication instantly. This of course creates a construct in which we are all "supposed to be" immediately available to respond instantly as well. And when we don't immediately respond? We create a space for a lot of broken loops for our conversational counterparts throughout the day. Additionally, there aren't just a few opportunities to miss a communication or not respond, but instead there are hundreds of opportunities to do so. With the unmitigated rise in the number of electronic communications we send and receive (as well as the ones we *don't* send) coupled with our cognitive need for closure and tendency toward the negative, we are in a perfect storm for agitation, anxiety, stress, distrust, and fearfulness. It's making us nuts, and no one is talking about it.

And unlike the Cuban Missile Crisis that was resolved in thirteen days, this crisis is not going anywhere anytime soon.

The Perfect Storm Meets a Global Pandemic: The Changing Ways We Communicate

Since I started writing this book, the world has changed seemingly overnight. The COVID-19 pandemic that began in China and then ravaged the world in just under three months' time has changed how all of us live, work, socialize, and communicate. And from the looks of it, it will continue to leave an indelible mark on how we proceed to connect and communicate for years to come.

Stuck in our homes quarantining and/or adapting to social distancing procedures, or what we are now calling a "new normal," most of us are all now completely dependent on electronic communications to carry on almost all of our basic human tasks. In the spring of 2020, the majority of the world (outside of essential workers) began working from home, educating their children from home, and even socializing from home. Zoom happy hour, anyone? All jokes aside, overnight, every single one of our personal and professional interactions became completely dependent on people getting back to us. We couldn't just pop over to a neighbor's house to ask for sugar. Those days were suddenly gone. We had to text or send an email and wait. We couldn't even walk over to our colleague's cubicle and have them look at the report we were working on together and get input; we had to send it to them in an email and wait. We couldn't just go and visit our aging parents in their home to check on them and see if they were healthy; we had to text, FaceTime, Zoom, or call, and you guessed it, wait. And what if they didn't answer? Were they lying on the floor somewhere in the house and couldn't reach us? Were they stuck in bed, struggling to breathe? With so much bad news catastrophized 24/7 by pundits, leaders, and news broadcasters, it was no wonder our brains jumped immediately to "my parents must be sick" when they didn't answer a text. Or, if we didn't hear back from a colleague right away, it seemed perfectly natural to think, "Oh, they hate what I've done!" or "They're not even working or trying as hard as I am to complete our work!" Or if the person you were dating before the pandemic stopped responding, it was clearly because of something you said in the last text you sent, not because they too were overwhelmed with all of their own incoming messages.

The very nature of electronic communications invites all this catastrophic thinking.

About Me

I am a media consultant. My career is developing messaging for political campaigns, nonprofit organizations, and corporations. My work started out with television and radio as the mediums for messaging, and now I use only digital communication.

My experience informs this book and provides the basis to assess digital Dyscommunication as well as provide you the tools to fix it. A key piece of my messaging work is using focus groups and polls to deeply understand an issue and to express the message clearly. In developing this book, I relied heavily on both qualitative and quantitative research. I conducted numerous interviews and surveys. All of this research was used to develop and validate the syndrome. I also reference dozens of studies in support.

This is a book about communication, why that communication breaks down, and what you can do to fix it. I have also utilized other authors with respect to the science and psychology in the book.

What to Expect

In the first part of the book, chapters 1-3, I go into more depth about what Dyscommunication Syndrome (DCS) is, what it isn't, and I expand on just how profound this crisis is in impacting our mental health, relationships, and workplaces. I also explain why it is so physically and mentally painful. In the second part of the book, chapters 4-7, I show how DCS manifests in real life, in dating, long-term relationships, families, and at work. In the third and final part of the book, I offer practical solutions to mitigate the harm it can have on our lives. I offer tested tactics so your messages are returned promptly. The best solution is to eradicate the problem. There are also tactics to reduce the impact of effects once Dyscommunication has happened, such as chasing a lost message and ways of reducing the negative loops of thinking while you wait. And finally, I show that negative loops of thinking occur in many other areas of your life besides an unreturned message, yet it's the same mechanism at work, which will give you further insight. Throughout the book, I've included reflection questions at the end of each chapter so you can assess your own reactions to DCS and help you recognize your own patterns in regard to how you respond when confronted with broken loops or unanswered communications. At the end of the book, I've included the survey data and demographic information as well as further reading and resources that I have found helpful. Along the way I'll be sharing stories of people whose lives have been affected by this syndrome or whose stories illustrate what role it has played in their life.

Ultimately, my sincere hope is that by the end of this book you, my readers, feel better and more at ease the next time you hear the words *I'll get back to you* followed by proverbial crickets. And while you're waiting for a response to that unreturned message and to close the broken loop but find yourself panicking anyway, I hope you remember this book and can stop and say: "Oh, this is just my DCS talking!"

I am a firm believer that shedding light where there is none is the single most powerful tool one can use to combat virtually anything, and I hope my book sheds a little blue light (a little digital humor) during some of your darkest moments. And like John F. Kennedy, I also believe that in every crisis we are called to be aware of the danger and recognize the opportunities. I share with you my understanding of the Dyscommunication crisis we're currently facing to not simply raise the legendary DEFCON-2 warning of its danger to our lives and well-being but also to highlight the many opportunities we have to find meaningful and lasting solutions.

CHAPTER 1

Understanding Dyscommunication Syndrome

It's 2 a.m. and Jane has now texted her teen son at least twenty times and has still received little to no response. She's panicked and irate. The first text she sent was at 11:30 p.m.

"Don't forget your curfew! See you at midnight. Have fun. Stay safe." Heart emoji. Prayer hands emoji.

Immediately, her son sends a crazy-face emoji.

"Okayyyyyy," she thinks aloud. "What does that mean? Is this teen-speak for 'won't forget curfew?' That he'll see me at midnight?" Or does this mean he thinks she's acting crazy? She'd feel a hell of a lot better if he had just given her a thumbs-up. "How hard is that? It's on the same keyboard!" she shouts to no one.

She doesn't want to seem overbearing, but this is his first night out with her car, and he only got his license two weeks ago. So, she tries to keep the text light to let him know she's "cool." She follows up with a sunglass emoji. "Two can play at this game," she says, satisfied with her emoji mastery.

She'd normally be asleep by 11:30 p.m., but she's determined to stay up to make sure her only son gets home safely from the homecoming dance he went to with his girlfriend, best friend Liam, and Liam's date.

She flips on a *Seinfeld* rerun to pass the time and keep her up, but she can't concentrate on anything else but her phone. At 11:45 p.m., Jane checks her phone again. Still no response.

"Hey bud, I know you're busy having fun. Just let me know when you leave the dance," followed by three heart emojis and a dancer emoji.

She drops the phone next to her and flips through the channels. She's starting to feel a quickening in her chest. "Why hasn't he texted? This isn't like him. He always has his phone on him." She opens Instagram. She sees his stories. At 9 p.m. he posted a video of his friends dancing in a packed high school gym. She smiles and comments with a heart. Seeing him, albeit digitally, makes her feel a bit better.

The minutes slowly tick by. She watches her phone clock. 11:47. 11:50. And nothing. She then remembers she has the Find My iPhone app installed on both their phones; she clicks it open and sees her son's phone is "Out of Range." The last place his phone tracked was the high school gym. "That's promising," she thinks. "Maybe he is on his way home. Service is spotty in certain areas." Though, for reasons beyond her, she can't help but begin to feel agitated and nervous.

She gets up and looks out the window and then at her phone. 11:55. "He'll be home any minute," she tries to tell herself. "It's not like him to ever be late. He'll be here."

At midnight she calls him. She doesn't want to text him if he's on the road. The call goes straight to voicemail. "Dammit, Tommy!" Jane yells at no one. "Answer your damn phone. That's why I pay for it!"

She begins to pace. She knows the high school is only ten minutes away. However, she's unsure of where his date lives. She remembers he also has to drive her home, as well as Liam and his date. "Maybe they were all talking and hanging out after the dance and lost track of time. It happens," she says, trying to talk herself down. "He'll be home any minute now." She resolves not to text him until 12:10. She can't wait any longer. At 12:09, she texts him.

"Hello??? Tommy? Curfew mean much? The dance was over at 11:30 p.m. Where are you????"

Nothing.

"Tommy? Just answer me. Are you okay?"

Over the course of the next hour, Jane paces the floor. She's at once incensed and worried. Then quite suddenly she becomes outraged with her son and starts making baseless accusations in her mind. *How could he be so irresponsible! He's so selfish. Keeping me up! He knows I have an early shift tomorrow morning. He never thinks of me. He's doing this on purpose. He's doing this just to piss me off, because I gave him a curfew in the first place. He would never do this to his father.*

The thought of her late husband sends a panic through her and her body shakes. *What if Tommy is hurt? What if he was in a car accident? What if someone attacked him on his way out of the school? What if he is dead?*

She texts him again, and again, and again.

"Tommy, I just need to hear that you're OK."

"Please, call me. Text me. Anything." Worried face emoji.

Suddenly, Jane remembers she has Tommy's friend Liam's phone number in her phone. Tommy had borrowed her phone the week before to call him when his own phone battery had died. She goes through her recent calls, finds the number, and texts Liam.

"Hi Liam! Jane here. Are you still with Tommy? Have you seen him?"

She waits. She sees the familiar three floating dots ... that mean he's texting back.

"Oh great! He's responding," Jane says.

But then suddenly the dots disappear. He stops writing. "Liam!" she screams at the phone. She decides to call him now. Liam sends her straight to voicemail.

"What the hell is going on!" Jane shouts. She's livid.

She stomps into the kitchen to make a cup of tea. She'd go out and find Tommy herself, but she remembers Tommy has her only car.

She decides to wait till 2 p.m. to call the police and hospitals.

In the meantime, she sends a flurry of voicemails and texts to Tommy.

In her mind, Jane believes without a shadow of doubt something terrible has happened to her son. She begins to cry at the thought that he is hurt or, worse, dead.

She calls her best friend. "Sorry to wake you, Sarah. But Tommy hasn't come home from the dance. I'm sure something terrible has happened!"

Sarah assures Jane that teenagers often lose track of time, and she's sure there is nothing to worry about. She tells Jane to call her in the morning, because she too is exhausted and needs to get back to sleep. Jane feels terrible for waking Sarah and is slightly ashamed and silently wonders *Maybe I am overreacting?*

When Jane sees red lights outside her window at 2:02 a.m., her stomach plunges. *She was right. Her son is dead.* She can't bring herself to open the door. She stands behind the door, fearful to open it.

When the door swings open and almost hits her in the face, she is stunned to see Tommy as he walks casually through the door.

"Oh my god! You're safe! You're alive!" Jane is furious and relieved and full of questions when she rushes at her son and hugs him.

"Chill, mom! Of course, I'm alive! Didn't Liam text you? Your car broke down and my phone battery died. Liam's dad came with his tow truck to get us and then helped us drop the girls off."

Just as Tom explains, Liam walks up behind Tom and admits, "Shoot! Dude! I totally forgot to text your mom back! My dad called to ask us where we were just as your mom called. Guess I forgot. Got distracted. Sorry, man."

Liam's dad then comes up behind the boys and explains to Jane he'd happily tow her car back to his shop and look at it in the morning. Jane agrees wearily. It's been a long night. Tommy then turns and asks if Liam can spend the night. Jane nods, too tired now to argue with her son and somewhat embarrassed. She thinks of all the texts, calls, and accusations that her son and Liam will wake up to. Her face reddens in shame.

"You both go on upstairs and get to bed," Jane says, relieved and exhausted.

It'd been a long night of thinking the worst.

What Jane went through is a classic case of DCS, which is, as we defined in the introduction, the result of unreturned messages causing a gap in the communication cycle and causing a broken loop inside her mind. Jane had every means available to her to get ahold of her son—phone, text, voicemail, direct message, social media, email, apps, and even alternate phone numbers of his friends. DCS, remember, isn't caused by miscommunication, but rather happens when communications are unreturned, ambiguous, or delayed. Dyscommunication can come (or not come) in many forms—emails, texts, direct messages on social media, and app-to-app messages, just like they did in Jane's case.

The delayed and unreturned texts and calls left Jane reeling. Then the ambiguous "…" from Liam made her imagine the worst. He knew something that she didn't, she assumed.

No matter what form it takes, Dyscommunication prevented Jane from gaining closure. Because her neocortex is wired to complete patterns, these broken loops caused a negative thinking spiral that followed a predictable DCS pattern.

Dyscommunication Syndrome: A Syndrome in Seven Parts

Elisabeth Kübler-Ross, psychiatrist and author of the best-selling book *On Death and Dying*, argued her theory that grief arrives in a pattern of five stages: denial, anger, bargaining, depression, and acceptance. My research has shown that Dyscommunication Syndrome has its own pattern that—in its full expression—has seven parts. The Kübler-Ross model is a famous example, but there are hundreds of lesser known "syndromes." A syndrome is simply a set of symptoms that happen to a person at a given time and because of particular circumstances. It's important to note that a "syndrome" is not always an exact "sequence." A syndrome is also not a disease. It does not apply to everybody. It does not happen to everyone who encounters a similar set of circumstances. We use the Kübler-Ross model only to underscore this particular syndrome by way of analogy. Dyscommunication is initiated because of a broken loop, and then it keeps repeating itself in a series of loops. In fact, 65 percent of people I surveyed say that broken loops of communication trigger negative thoughts, and these negative thoughts tend to repeat in a cycle. Unfortunately for us, however, this cycle has a downward trajectory.

It all starts when a loop of communication is broken. From there, the following seven stages occur.

1. <u>Anxiety and agitation</u>
This first stage generally starts with repetitive thoughts that are benign enough: "Has he written back yet?" And then, ten

minutes later, "What about now?" Jane checking her phone every minute and finding it hard to focus on anything else is a telltale sign that DCS is ramping up. Pretty quickly, though, those banal wonderings switch over to thoughts that are full of fearfulness.

2. <u>Taking it personally</u>

After a varying amount of general, anxious thoughts, the ego kicks in and tries to make the broken loop into evidence that there is something wrong with you. This is often accompanied by thoughts such as "This always happens to me." "There's something about me that keeps people at a distance." "I should have seen this coming." Or in Jane's case, she accuses her son of doing this "on purpose" just to "piss" her off because she gave him a curfew.

3. <u>Resentment and distrust</u>

What happens next is that we start to have thoughts that we are likely to be ashamed to admit having to someone else. We begin developing theories that, if we said them out loud, would sound paranoid and downright delusional. "She's probably telling someone right now how she doesn't want to be friends anymore." "Why do I even bother putting myself out there for people? They all suck." There is some shallow comfort in finding someone or something else to take the blame for our uncomfortable feelings, but it comes at the cost of assuming the worst in people and losing sight of our innate empathy for and connection to people we are in some form of relationship with.

4. Catastrophizing

Because we so strongly crave a narrative that has an end point, we will, at some point, create our own ending. Generally, because we are in full-on fearfulness mode, what we imagine as a plausible reason why the loop was broken will be a worst-case scenario. "I bet she's at a party right now telling everyone what a loser I am; not only am I losing this one friend, I'm going to lose them all." Really, at this stage, nothing is too "out there" to contemplate. Even though the worst-case scenario is painful and stressful to contemplate, it's nevertheless a concrete period at the end of the otherwise incomplete sentence. Jane begins thinking the worst—that her son is dead. There is nothing more final.

5. Possibly doing something you regret

There are a wide variety of choices here that can vary from:

- Self-medicating with food, alcohol, or drugs.
- Gossiping (venting to friends by saying something like "Who does she think she is anyway?").
- Leaving awkward phone messages or sending angry emails.
- Driving past their house with your headlights turned off or, at the very least, checking out their social media feeds to make sure they're not sick or dead. (Hey, who among us hasn't resorted to some level of stalking at some point, even if said stalking is virtual?)
- Thinking about self-destruction.
- Or, in the case of Kennedy and Khrushchev, blowing up the world—or our own lives.

Even if you aren't actually *doing* any of these things, you are likely to at least be thinking about them. Jane embarrassingly calls a friend in the middle of the night, contacts Tommy's friend Liam, and even makes all kinds of accusations over voicemail to her son and to Liam.

6. Inability to talk yourself down

Because the brain can't tolerate an incomplete pattern, your thoughts will tend to just keep looping. If you manage to tell yourself it's not about you and there's nothing you can do but wait and be patient, at some point, the fearfulness will start creeping back in, and you'll be back to one of the previous stages, whether that's agitation or catastrophizing. By the end of the evening, Jane's in a full-blown spiral, convinced of the worse.

7. Feeling ashamed

Whether the loop ever finally gets closed or not, often DCS ends with you feeling badly about your own reaction. These feelings can remain unresolved, particularly since there are so many opportunities to experience DCS daily. As a result, your "new normal" is a little bit more fearful and non-trusting than it would have been in the days before smartphones and digital communications became so ubiquitous, unless you take steps to acknowledge and address your own Dyscommunication. After Jane sees her son is well, immediately she recalls all the calls and accusations and feels embarrassed for overreacting.

Until the mind can complete the broken loop, it will continue to create its own narrative on why the communication has not been completed, spinning down a spiral that leads, invariably, to shame. Shame that the Dyscommunication happened (*Why don't people respect/understand/care about me?*), and shame that we got so worked up about it. And the crusher is, research has found that 90 percent of the time the Dyscommunication *has nothing to do with you*!

Jane's experience with her son Tommy was just one of many that day. At work she sends emails all day and leaves voice messages and waits for responses. She manages her personal relationships with friends via technology as well. She checks in on Facebook and Instagram. She has text thread groups with her parents, one with her sisters, one with her girlfriends from college, one with her work colleagues, and another with her book club. She also communicates daily with the boyfriend she's been seeing off and on for two years. Sometimes communication with him can be fraught, since he is divorced and busy with two kids as well. Daily, Jane is dealing with hundreds of broken loops—unreturned, unanswered, delayed, and ambiguous responses. No wonder Jane is exhausted and at her wit's end by 2 a.m. Who wouldn't be?

Jane isn't alone. All of us can relate to Jane in some way. Who hasn't gone from zero to catastrophe in a few short hours in this digital age?

Since most of us haven't really thought about the dramatic role unreturned messages have been playing in our daily lives, I want you to take an inventory of sorts of just how DCS might actually be impacting your overall mental and physical well-being on any given day. The following brief assessment will help you get an objective look at how much of an effect Dyscommunication has on your life and how to clearly determine the scope and impact that digital communications may have on your own life. Most of us aren't even aware of this crisis hiding in plain sight in the palms of our hands.

Self-Assessment Tool #1: How Much Do You Rely on Digital Communication on a Daily Basis?

1. List all your inboxes—email accounts, voicemail, messaging apps, social media accounts.
2. How many emails, texts, voicemails, and direct messages do you receive in a day?
3. How many emails, texts, voicemails, and direct messages do you send in a day?
4. How many emails in your inbox are currently waiting for your response?
5. How many texts?
6. How many voicemails?
7. How many hours a day do you find yourself communicating with others digitally?
8. What is the average time you wait for a response for a text? For an email? Direct message?
9. What would you consider an appropriate amount of time to respond or to receive a response to a digital communication?
10. Is there a certain type of digital communication you prefer? Why?
11. How many texts, emails, or messages do you leave unanswered?

CHAPTER 2

The Current
Dyscommunication Crisis

So Many Texts, So Little Time

Bob is on a Zoom call, about to close on an important deal with a potential client. He is in the second hour of tense negotiations when he glances over at his phone on the desk and sees a flurry of texts popping in from his longtime friend John. Bob rolls his eyes. John is notorious for sending multiple texts to ask a single question, just to get Bob's attention. *Good ol' John*, Bob thinks, laughing at John's usual insistence for a reply by using one-word texts in a series, filling his entire home screen:

> *Today is the day.*
> Depressed face emoji.
> *Bob?*
> *You there?*
> *Whatchya doin?*

Have a minute to chat?
You there?

Bob doesn't even bother opening the text thread. This is how John texts. He often sends Bob texts throughout the day asking him all kinds of questions about shows they both watch, updating Bob about sports-related news, or sending him memes he finds funny. Bob is used to getting a lot of texts from John, some of which are just emojis, so he doesn't think it's an emergency. It rarely is. Besides, he can't look away from his client on Zoom. He doesn't want to break what little "eye contact" he has with this potential client, and he wants to make sure this client feels just as heard and understood as he would if they were in person. He really needs this income right now. Things have been slow for him all month, since the pandemic all but shut his industry down. He isn't going to try to multitask and risk losing a major sale by picking up the phone to quickly type that he would text John back later. First, Bob thinks, he doesn't want his client to suspect he's not paying attention. Second, he doesn't feel that he *needs* to respond to John immediately anyway. *Just because someone isn't busy and can text you in the middle of the day, doesn't mean I'm not busy. I'm not at everyone else's beck and call*, Bob thinks. He flips the phone over and promises himself to get back to John after the Zoom meeting. As soon as the Zoom meeting is over and Bob closes the sale, he's exhausted. He gets up to stretch and grabs a beer from the fridge and then steps outside for some fresh air. He sees his wife and daughter playing on the swing and joins them for a bit. His wife says she is hungry and doesn't feel like cooking and wonders if Bob would mind running out for some takeout. Bob says sure. By the time dinner is over and his wife takes their daughter up to bed, Bob finally looks at his texts. There are over fifty texts from John now. Bob reads through them. He can't believe what he is reading. His friend of over twenty-five years is calling him selfish. He's accusing him of purposely screwing him over. He accuses Bob of never being there for him. Bob can tell that John is, by all accounts, livid. Bob is incredulous. *What the hell? Where did this come from, John? Because I didn't text you back ASAP? I have my own life. I can't be tethered to my phone to text you back!* Bob thinks angrily.

Bob tries to settle down and then racks his brain, thinking of reasons why John would say such things. Bob hesitates to call back. After all, he's doesn't want to engage with John when he's obviously so upset. Bob, exhausted now himself with the whole ordeal, is suddenly feeling short-tempered and is in no mood to deal with John in this state either. So, he decides to hold off responding. *I'll just wait till morning to call him back,* Bob thinks. *I don't have time for this shit.*

Before heading to bed, however, Bob opens Facebook and sees John's tribute to his late wife who died from cancer five years ago today. *Oh god,* Bob thinks and his stomach drops. *I totally forgot what day it was!* Between work, the stressful call, his wife, daughter, dinner, and, well, his own life, Bob forgot what an important day it was for John and their usual plans to go to a local pub together on this day to commemorate John's wife. Bob instantly feels terrible. In fact, he feels sick to his stomach. He texts John, explains what his day was like, apologizes, and lets John know he's available to talk tomorrow.

But John doesn't text Bob back immediately either. He's too angry his friend forgot him (or ignored him for all he knows) and too ashamed about his own actions—for saying terrible things and making baseless accusations. He knows Bob is starting a business, struggling financially, working from home during a pandemic, and taking care of his own family. John knows he should have cut Bob some slack, but in the moment, it felt like Bob was purposefully ignoring him. John has lost so many friends over the past few years because they didn't know how to cope with his grief over losing his wife, and he thought now Bob was just following suit. John feels depressed. He is suddenly plunged into a deep state of self-loathing, loneliness, and despair and is even contemplating a form of self-destruction. Meanwhile, Bob, who is now also waiting for a response, is left to assume John hates him and is unwilling to forgive him.

The two men don't speak or text for several days. As the days go by, Bob begins to spiral as well. Not hearing from John is upsetting Bob now. He becomes angry and accusatory as well and doesn't think he even wants to be friends with someone so "irrational" as John anymore. Since he isn't talking to John, he has no idea how depressed, lonely, and isolated John feels. And Bob is, of course, unaware of the irony that John was feeling the same way as Bob does today just a few days ago when he didn't respond to the initial texts. Meanwhile, John also feels terrible for saying such horrible things to Bob, but he is too proud to say he's sorry and too depressed to do anything about it. Their friendship is on the brink. It may, in fact, never recover. And even worse, their mental and physical health are in peril as well.

Why? As silly as it seems, it all comes down to an unreturned message and acute cases of DCS.

▍ Relationships on the Brink of Crisis

The Dyscommunication crisis has reached epic proportions as a result of society's move from communicating primarily either in person or by phone to communicating via email or texts. Under the former communication paradigm, there was a direct feedback loop—you spoke to another person in real time on the phone or in person. If something were unclear you could immediately ask a question and resolve any ambiguity. This process was fostered by the ability to see body language and/or hear voice intonation, which provided emotional feedback. In our current communication reality, there is no immediate feedback loop and little emotional communication. Not only is there a delay between question and answer, there's also often confusion about the meaning of the response. Digital communication leaves us with dozens, even hundreds of broken loops every day. We are left always wondering if our message has been understood and waiting indefinitely for it to be returned.

Dyscommunication is also a natural consequence of sheer volume: The average American sends 40 and receives 126 emails per day, spends two hours a day on an average of three different social media sites (all of which have their own direct messaging functions), and sends and receives an average of 72 texts a day (unless they are eighteen to twenty-four years old, in which case that number rises to 128 texts sent and received a day). That is hundreds of opportunities for Dyscommunication.

On top of the quantity of messages we're sending and receiving—or *not* sending, because, after all, who has time to respond to 126 emails and 72 texts in one day?—our conversational style and mores are ambiguous. No matter how many emojis you use, you can't really convey or read tone or body language via electronic communication. This lack of physical context means there are more opportunities than ever to misread the other person's intent. Beyond that, during a face-to-face or even a voice-to-voice conversation (remember that quaint notion of the phone call?), we have been trained to expect a response to what we say *within seconds.* But now—despite the fact that 90 percent of cellphone users "frequently" have their phone with them, and 76 percent "rarely" or "never" turn their phones off—we typically have to wait minutes if not hours or even days to get a response to our messages. Sometimes this is a deliberate power play, and sometimes a simple truth that the person we're communicating with is busy or forgot, because she has all those other texts, emails, and direct messages to respond to. Sometimes people are just downright annoyed by the constant intrusions of texts and emails in their day. Sometimes it's the combination of all three, as in the case of Bob and John. At first Bob purposefully ignored John's messages, because he was both annoyed by the sheer quantity of the messages and the intrusion in his busy day. And then he got sidetracked by several other pressing priorities. But as the day went by, the messages just got away from him, and he completely forgot to respond. It doesn't matter though why Bob didn't return the message, because for John, who was waiting on the other end—it only mattered that he didn't. The unreturned message and response limbo were wreaking havoc on his psychological state. John went rapidly through the stages of DCS from taking it personally, to catastrophizing, contemplating doing something as rash as suicide, and finally to shame, all in the course of a day. John and Bob had been friends for years, but their seemingly solid relationship had reached its breaking point over a matter of hours.

John and Bob's relationship is a microcosm of what is happening all over, every day. In homes, workplaces, and relationships (romantic and platonic), people are suffering and causing serious harm to others—and of course themselves—simply because they don't understand what is happening to them when they are engaging in these communications.

Our Physical and Mental Health: The National Crisis

Emails. Texts. DMs. Slack messages. Facebook and Instagram comments. LinkedIn requests. Think about how you answered the assessment questions in Chapter 1, where you listed all the ways people are reaching out to you during the day. It's overwhelming, right? This influx of inputs means we don't even typically have time to read an entire email: we scan and then fill in our own blanks, which typically means we jump to conclusions. And read the attachments? Forget about it.

DCS caused by unreturned messages isn't just a personal experience; it's a national crisis. When I surveyed Americans, I found that 64 percent believe the escalating use of emails and texts causes psychological damage and is a direct cause of their anxiety. When asked what is the cause of negative psychological impact of emails and texts, 74 percent of Americans say it is due to the sheer volume, 66 percent attribute it to unreturned texts and emails, and 50 percent say it is because of the ambiguity of the content of the emails and texts. And 72 percent said that an unreturned text or email left them reeling, resulting in negative loop thinking. And, not surprisingly, 70 percent admit that once the email or text has been returned, their catastrophic thoughts turned out to be inaccurate. Just as in the case of John—his friend wasn't being selfish; he was just busy and stressed about closing a deal.

But John's response isn't atypical. This kind of catastrophic thinking is happening all around us. We are drowning in a sea of messages. This isn't just bad for our productivity, it's bad for our mental health, which in turn affects our physical health. According to the National Institute for Mental Health (NIMH), long-term stress can seriously affect your overall health. The current Dyscommunication crisis is wreaking havoc on our daily stress and anxiety levels. Most of us are unaware of the silent toll it is taking on both our bodies and minds. According to the NIMH, long-term stress is much more dangerous than acute stress—such as a sudden traumatic event. Why? Because long-term, unchecked stress is constantly threatening the body's immune, digestive, cardiovascular, sleep, and reproductive systems. Because the stress is quite literally ongoing and ever present, the NIMH says "the body never receives a clear signal to return to normal functioning."[1] With chronic stress, various chemical and hormonal reactions ensue and ultimately disturb all our major systems. As a result, some people may experience digestive symptoms (like Bob, when he felt sick to his stomach), while others may have headaches, sleeplessness, sadness, anger, irritability, and depression (like John).

You can likely intrinsically sense that stress isn't good for you because of the way it makes your body feel—clenched muscles, shallow breathing, headaches, indigestion, poor sleep. But stress, particularly chronic stress, has effects that reach down to our very core. Among the most pernicious ways that stress eats away at our well-being are:

- **Impacts gene expression.** The hormones your body produces as a result of stress can turn on or turn off genes that are responsible for a wide range of functions, including how well your immune system works,[2] how much fat you store, how quickly you age, and whether you will or will not develop cancer.

- **Contributes to chronic mild inflammation.** Many of the chemicals released when you are under stress, including C-reactive protein, trigger the immune system to produce an inflammatory response. Inflammation in and of itself is a helpful action of the immune system for an acute stressor—it delivers extra blood cells and immune cells to the site of an injury, for example. But when it is consistently activated, even at low levels, your body is always on guard to protect you from invaders or to deliver the building blocks of healing to an injury. When there is no invader or injury, and the inflammation is never fully switched off, the body essentially begins attacking itself, ultimately creating the conditions for disease. Mild inflammation is believed to be the primary reason why chronic stress is associated with up to 90 percent of chronic diseases, including heart disease, diabetes, non-alcoholic fatty liver disease, depression, Alzheimer's, Parkinson's, and cancer.[3]

- **Impairs brain function.** Some of the chemicals released as a result of stress—particularly psychological stress—can cause physical damage to your brain, particularly the hippocampus, which is responsible for memory storage and retention. Research has found that stress reduces memory formation and recall, prevents neurons from growing stronger, and even reduces the overall volume of the hippocampus.[4]

- **Disrupts gut health.** Stress also has negative impacts on what's known as your second brain. When in fight or flight mode, your body sends chemical messages that slow digestion. When the stress is never fully abated, this can lead to constipation and reduced ability to purge things the body no longer needs, including toxins and hormones, such as estrogen. Stress also contributes to the overgrowth of bad bacteria, such as yeast, in the gut. With an unchecked population of unfriendly bacteria, the seals between the cells that line your intestines can weaken, allowing undigested food to leave the GI tract and go into the bloodstream, which then serves as another trigger for inflammation. Poor gut health has a direct tie to mental health, too, as many neurotransmitters, such as serotonin, are primarily manufactured by the friendly bacteria in your gut. When your neurotransmitter levels are off, it can contribute to anxiety and depression.

- **Hurts your heart health.** Chronic stress has been shown to contribute to thicker artery walls, impaired endothelial function, and calcification of the coronary artery.[5, 6] When you consider that heart disease is the number one killer of women—responsible for one out of three female deaths, more than all cancers combined— you see just how high a toll the stress of DCS can exact.

In addition, chronic stress contributes to lost sleep, moodiness, and difficulty focusing. It negatively impacts our enjoyment and our effectiveness in all parts of life.

Continued and sustained exposure to stress contributes to all the major serious health problems currently plaguing Americans at record-setting rates. Heart disease, high blood pressure, diabetes, mental disorders such as depression or anxiety, and suicide rates are all on the upswing. And who is using digital technology more than anyone? Teenagers. The unreturned messages are affecting them especially so. According to research from the Johns Hopkins Bloomberg School of Public Health, adolescents are facing rates of depression that are increasing at an alarming rate—between 2005 and 2014 alone, the odds that an adolescent will suffer from clinical depression (which is more than just the blues, but a debilitating disease that can make even getting out of bed difficult) grew by 37 percent. Researchers aren't the only ones seeing this trend—teens themselves acknowledge it too. A 2019 study from the Pew Research Center found that a whopping 70 percent of teenagers admit that they see anxiety and depression as major challenges for them and their peers—more so than bullying, alcohol, or drugs.[7] Anxiety and depression led the pack of concerns in teens no matter what income bracket they were in and no matter whether they lived in a city, suburb, or rural town.

Anxiety and depression, particularly among teens, can turn deadly as adolescents—who are more finely attuned to their place in their peer groups and more attached to their digital communications than any other demographic—think about or attempt suicide. In fact, the American Academy of Pediatrics found that between 2008 and 2015, hospital visits for thinking about or attempting suicide doubled.[8]

These numbers have risen in an eerily similar pattern to the increase in the number of cellphone subscribers over the same time period: 229.6 million in 2005, 274.2 million in 2009, 382.3 million in 2015, and 395.8 million in 2017.[9] (Keep in mind that the U.S. population in 2017 was 325.7 million, meaning there was more than one cellphone subscription for each and every American.)

Teens aren't the only ones who feel the emotional pain of broken loops, of course. In 2017, a survey of one thousand U.S. adults by the American Psychiatric Association found that nearly two thirds were "extremely or somewhat anxious about health and safety for themselves and their families and more than a third are more anxious overall than last year," with millennials being the most anxious generation surveyed.[10] In 2018, they repeated the poll, and self-reported anxiety had risen by an additional 5 percent, with millennials again leading the way.[11]

It's not just America: in a 2017 report, the U.K. Council for Psychotherapy published a report on the mental health of working adults that found that "workers reporting anxiety and depression have risen by nearly a third in the last four years."[12]

Now I am not saying unreturned messages *alone* are the cause of this current major health crises. However, the anxiety and stress responses caused by the broken loops that are a direct result of unreturned messages certainly aren't helping anyone who is already suffering from chronic mental and physical health issues. And most people have no idea where the majority of their stress and anxiety come from in the first place. I believe there are two obvious culprits—money and communication. Since this book is about communication, or the lack thereof, I'll save the topic of money for another day (and possibly another book).

For the sake of understanding just how much unreturned communications and the anxiety and stress created by said communications are affecting *you* on a daily basis, I've included the following assessment so you can clearly see just how much this silent crisis is impacting your own life.

Self-Assessment Tool #2: How Much Does Digital Communication Affect Your Mental and Physical Health on a Daily Basis?

Ask yourself:

- On a scale of 1-10, with 1 being so overcome with negative emotion that you can't function in your daily life, to 10 being absolutely elated, how do you feel when:
  - Someone doesn't return your email within two hours
  - Someone doesn't return your email within eight hours
  - Someone doesn't return your email within twenty-four hours
  - You don't respond to someone's email text within two hours
  - You don't respond to someone's email text within eight hours
  - You don't respond to someone's email text within twenty-four hours
- When you wake up in the middle of the night, what types of thoughts do you have about:
  - The communication you sent that wasn't answered
  - The communication you received that you haven't responded to
  - Whether the communication you sent was understood
  - What someone said to you in a message that you received

- How many times a day do you check your phone or inbox in hopes of finding that your communication has been returned?
- How do you feel physically after checking messages and finding that your own message is left unreturned or received an ambiguous answer?

CHAPTER 3

Why Dyscommunication Syndrome Is So Painful

Melanie and Kim have been friends for seven years; they shared a cubicle in their late twenties and became quite close. Now that they've gone on to work for other companies, and Kim has gotten married and had a baby, the two don't get together all that often, although they still consider each other close friends.

Melanie and Kim keep up their friendship by commenting on each other's social media posts and staying in touch mostly via text. Melanie shares funny moments from her dating life. Kim sends baby photos. They give each other perspective when one of them faces a challenging situation at work. They know they aren't as tight as they once were, but they are proud of keeping their bond strong despite the different tracks their lives have taken.

One Thursday morning, Melanie gets some great news: she is being offered a promotion at work. That same afternoon, she receives a call from a recruiter about a dream job at a new company. Melanie texts Kim that evening. "OMG! I have work dish to share!" she writes. Knowing Kim is probably putting her kid to bed, she also writes, "Know you're probably embroiled in bedtime…when's a good time to talk?" Kim doesn't write back that night. Melanie thinks it's weird, but maybe her friend had fallen asleep when she put the baby down and will call her tomorrow morning. No big deal.

The next morning when Melanie is getting ready for work, Kim still hasn't written back. *That's weird,* Melanie thinks, *maybe she's traveling for work and I just don't know it?* The thought gives her a little pang—a physical reminder that the two aren't as close as they once were.

At work that morning, Melanie has two meetings back-to-back, so she doesn't even have a chance to check her phone until almost 11 a.m. Still nothing. *Okay, this is getting weird. What's going on with her?* Melanie wonders. *I hope everything's okay.* She decides to check Kim's social media accounts to see if Kim has posted anything that would explain why she isn't writing back, but there are no updates.

Even though she tries to distract herself, Melanie spends the rest of the workday checking her phone every few minutes. Each time there is no text from Kim, she gets a little more agitated. *Is she tired of being friends with me?* she wonders. By the end of the day, Melanie's head is throbbing, and that pang she'd felt in her stomach earlier is now constant, as if she's swallowed something heavy.

Melanie can't dwell on the feeling for long though, because she is meeting her newish boyfriend Mike right after work. She thinks maybe a drink and a diversion will do her some good.

While they are out, Mike raises the possibility of moving in together. After they talk about whether they should move in to one of their existing apartments or find a new place together, Mike goes to use the bathroom. The first thing Melanie does is fire off a quick text to Kim that says, "HOLY SHIT crazy stuff is happening here! Where are you?? Hope everything's OK. Call me when you can!"

Later that night, Melanie and Mike go back to his place. While he's in the bathroom brushing his teeth, Melanie checks her phone. Nothing from Kim. *WHY ISN'T SHE WRITING ME BACK?* she thinks. *When I talk to her, I'm going to have to give her a piece of my mind; this isn't what friends do!*

Luckily, Mike is happy to distract her from any more rumination that night.

On Saturday morning, as soon as she wakes up, Melanie takes her phone in to the bathroom with her, thinking surely Kim has written back by now. Still nothing, though. *Oh God, what if something's wrong with the baby?!*, Melanie thinks to herself. Melanie can feel her mind spinning, her breath getting shallow, and her face getting hot.

Tired of feeling agitated, Melanie decides to go to yoga to try and calm herself down.

Around noon, on her way home from yoga, Melanie calls Kim. No answer. She tries to sound cool as she leaves a message, "Hey, it's me. Would love to talk to you when you get a sec! You all still alive over there? Ha ha." After she hangs up, Melanie starts running through a list of things that could have gone wrong. *Maybe she was in a car accident. Or maybe she and her husband are in a huge fight.* Trying to get a grip on herself,

Melanie decides to clean her apartment. But she just can't let it go. She keeps checking her phone and wondering what the reason could possibly be why Kim hasn't reached out yet.

That night, Melanie has plans to see a movie with Mike and another couple. Even though it's a sci-fi action movie, chock full of special effects, explosions, and plot twists, Melanie can't settle in and get lost in the plot. Not hearing from Kim has officially entered the territory of "something is not right." She's in full-on anxiety mode, her thoughts running in an endless loop trying to concoct an explanation that makes sense why Kim is suddenly AWOL.

Melanie tries to be engaged in the conversation at the bar after the movie, but she can't muster much enthusiasm, even when Mike tells the table that Melanie has gotten a promotion and a call from the recruiter. She keeps a portion of her attention on the phone that she has sitting on the table, willing it to light up.

On Sunday morning, there's still no word from Kim. By now, Melanie is starting to take it personally. *Did I do something to piss her off and she never told me? Seven years of friendship and this is how she wants to treat me? Why is she doing this to me??*

By Sunday night, Melanie's thoughts have veered into resentment. *I always text her back,* she tells herself. *I'm always there for her, and she doesn't care about me. I've been fooling myself.* She tries to distract herself by watching a few episodes of the new season of her favorite show before getting in bed. But once she's there, she still finds her thoughts churning over all the various reasons Kim's gone rogue.

Maybe Kim was in a car accident, and now she's in a coma. She shakes her head as if she's trying to knock the thoughts loose.

She's got a new life now, but she doesn't have the guts to tell me we've grown apart. I guess I'm being dumped by my own friend! That's just great. Some way to treat a friend.

The next morning, Melanie starts fantasizing about leaving a nasty message on Kim's voicemail. She imagines everything she'd say: "You know, you may think that I haven't been a good friend to you, but do you know how many times I sat and listened to you talk about naps, and diapers, and baby poop? You think I care? You have become so self-absorbed I don't even know why I expected you to be excited for me!" She doesn't do it, but somehow just thinking about it is comforting.

Melanie is in a full-blown spiral.

During the day, every time Melanie has a quiet moment to herself, she feels the pang of upset—wondering what happened, feeling like she's been dumped by someone she thought was a friend. At night, she has trouble sleeping, waking up in the middle of the night ruminating more about what could possibly be going on with Kim. She spends her waking moments ping-ponging between worry, anger, mistrust, and a vindictiveness that shocks her when she goes so far as to think, *I'm going to call her husband and tell him what a horrible friend Kim is, and how she's a bad role model for their kid.*

All the while, Melanie's trying to keep her head clear enough to navigate her job opportunities and to be real with Mike about her upset without casting a pall over their decision to move in together.

Two weeks later, Kim finally calls. Melanie's in a meeting and can't pick up, so Kim leaves a message that begins, "Melanie, I'm so sorry." She goes on to share that her mom has spent the last two and a half weeks in the hospital with a heart infection. Between work, the baby, and navigating the health care system, Kim had completely ignored her phone. "I just couldn't take care of one more thing," she says in her message. "Something had to give, and it was my friends. She's home now and feeling a lot better. I'm so, so sorry, I think you had some important stuff going on too, please call me. If you don't hate me, I want to hear all about it."

In the end, all of Melanie's upset—while perfectly understandable—was a party in her own head. Kim wasn't in a coma, nor was she an evil person. She just got sideswiped by life for a couple weeks.

But Melanie's emotional roller coaster isn't over just yet— now she's ashamed at her own reaction. *I can't believe I had these crazy, mean thoughts about my friend, especially when she was going through such a hard time.*

Granted, this is a dramatic example of exactly how communications gone wrong can wreak havoc on our relationships, our well-being, and our lives, but most of us have at least one story that's of a similar intensity.

There are variations of this story of different intensities that happen on a daily basis because it's a physical impossibility that every single one of the texts, emails, and direct messages get answered in a timely fashion. The truth is, experiencing a delayed response—and all the emotions that stirs up—is a fact of life. But when you can recognize the emotional roller coaster for what it is and anticipate its turns and dips, you can better manage your own reaction. This is again a classic example of the stages of DCS we outlined in the previous chapter.

First, there is the waiting for a response. As soon as Melanie sends that first text, whether she is aware of it or not, the first loop has been broken. Her neocortex, or the advanced mind's pattern finder, goes into alert, looking for an input that will help close the broken loop. She reaches out continuously and has no immediate resolution in any case, hence even more broken loops. In the period between sending her texts and waiting for responses, Melanie goes through a cascade of emotions. The broken loops make her feel, well, "loopy" and out of sorts, though she can't articulate why. She is distracted, frustrated, and unable to concentrate even when she is supposed to be relaxing and having fun with her boyfriend. She feels physical sensations—likened to a panic attack—and even tries to do some yoga to calm herself down. She also takes the messages personally. Clearly Kim not responding means Melanie has done something wrong. Then comes catastrophizing, when the crisis has reached its proverbial DEFCON-1 level. An immediate threat is imminent. Melanie feels like she is "dumped." She can't sleep. She ping-pongs between worry, anger, mistrust, and vindictiveness. She then thinks of doing something she'll regret, like calling Kim's husband and saying hurtful things. Finally, at stage seven, once the broken loop is finally closed and Melanie finally hears from Kim, the final stage sets in—shame. Melanie is embarrassed about overreacting.

Dyscommunication Syndrome Is a Normal Response to Broken Loops

As I mentioned in the introduction, at the root of the emotional roller coaster that is DCS is a primary function of our brain—pattern recognition and completion. This fundamental piece of how our brain processes the world is what helps us make sense of the information and circumstances we are continually presented with. It's how you discern that a certain set of shapes and strokes forms a word that you recognize, how you tell if a person is friendly or a threat, and how you tell where you are.

Scanning for patterns is just what our brains do automatically, like breathing. Higher order functions, such as retaining facts, performing calculations, and implementing logic, all take much more effort and training, like salsa dancing. At all times, beneath the level of your awareness, your brain is taking in some input, discerning the pattern it falls into, and predicting what will happen next. Then it stays attuned to see that the pattern you predicted does in fact happen.

When we pour our heart into a text—or even ask a simple question—and don't hear back right away, the brain starts spinning, seeking to complete the pattern for as long as the communication loop remains open.

We don't just recognize completion of a pattern; we crave it. "Closure" is a word that gets thrown around a lot when discussing breakups and other emotionally upsetting events, but it's not just lingo, it's a physiological drive. And that's where we can get tripped up and veer off into the full emotional roller coaster. With a text that goes unreturned or a digital conversation that isn't clearly resolved, because the communication is ambiguous and lacks visual patterns of body language and auditory patterns of tone, the typical pattern of communication is left incomplete. It becomes a broken loop.

An unreturned text or ambiguous email prevents us from being able to close the loop. When a pattern doesn't have an end point, or the end point is different than how we anticipated the pattern would go, we are confronted with a broken loop. Like a bird with no place to land, our thoughts will keep flapping until the pattern we've encountered concludes. Our minds can't rest.

This need for completing a broken loop is why you can have an involved, animated conversation with a friend about a song you both loved, but when the name of the artist escapes you, you feel compelled to pause the conversation until you can look the name of the artist up on your phone. It's also why you can't stop wondering why you haven't heard back from someone yet… your neurons are seeking resolution.

To better understand how the interruption of a pattern can lead to emotional upset, let's talk about clowns—creatures that often instill fear in kids and adults alike. Think of the murderous clown that lived under Carol Anne's bed in *Poltergeist* in 1982, Twisty the Clown in the fourth season of *American Horror Story* in 2014, and Pennywise in the 2017 movie *It*, which was based on a 1986 Stephen King novel and 1990 movie of the same name. In 2016, these creepy characters jumped off the screen and into real life as fiendish-looking clowns who started showing up in many different settings in the U.S. and around the world—lurking menacingly on the edges of woods, shouting at other drivers from behind the wheels of cars, and even patrolling playgrounds and graveyards.

What is it about clowns that makes them so frightening? According to a 2016 study, it is primarily their ambiguity that makes them creepy. They have two eyes, two ears, a nose, a mouth, two arms, and two legs, so they are clearly humans. But they also, with their drawn-on expressions, ashen white faces, and bulbous red noses, deviate from the pattern of what a human is expected to look like. In addition to their out-of-the-norm appearance, clowns behave mischievously—you don't know if they'll give you a balloon, throw a pie in your face, or try to kill you. We don't know how the pattern will end, and for many of us, that triggers anxiety, or even outright fear and trauma. In fact, coulrophobia—the scientific name for a fear of clowns derived from the Greek word for "those who walk on stilts"—is listed in the psychology bible, the DSM.

Seeking to discern patterns is "a default mode network that's happening all the time, even though you're not aware of it," says Steve Schlozman, M.D., an assistant professor of psychiatry at Harvard Medical School. "It helps us relatively quickly size up what we think we're seeing and search our memory banks for something similar so we can make sense of it and use that information to decide how to take the next step. When you encounter something that doesn't quite fit the pattern, you start working hard to make it fit. And if you can't it's really unsettling."[1]

And that unsettled feeling can last long after you first encounter the disrupted pattern. That's because your brain naturally stays focused on a broken loop, leaving less attention open for moving on to new things.

What makes us so focused on broken loops? One reason is that in order to retain information in short-term memory, you need to keep rehearsing them. While this happens beneath the level of your conscious awareness, it does require cognitive effort. The more broken loops you are holding in your mind at one time, the more effort required, and the more you will tend to revisit each open item in search of some relief. With the sheer number of unresolved communications any of us has in any given moment, this stockpile of broken loops can easily lead to obsessive thoughts.

Those thoughts tend to be pretty dark in nature and get darker as time goes on. Why? In an unconscious effort to complete the narrative and close the broken loop, your mind will tend to fill in the blanks with negative conjectures. It's not your fault; you're not just an anxious personality or a Negative Nellie. Humans are subject to what's known as a *negativity bias*—a predilection to dwell on negative things more than positive things. The negativity bias helped us survive when we were still living in clans on the savannas; it made us hyper-focused on remembering which berries made us sick or what conditions tended to make animals stampede. What kept us alive centuries ago still guides our thoughts and encourages us to fill in any blanks we encounter with negative explanations.

Thanks to the negativity bias, a thought such as *She's ten minutes late, maybe she got hit by a bus* becomes perfectly rational. It also means we end up suffering dozens of imagined catastrophes a day—a slow death by a thousand paper cuts.

On a more philosophical level, a broken loop offends our perpetual desire for meaning, understanding, and connection.

It becomes a story with no end, and so we seek to create our own ending in the hopes that then our minds will be able to rest. Even though the ending we create is more likely to make our banal little story into a grand tragedy—that feels better to us than not knowing how things will end.

The Result of the Problem Is Not Fear

Since we are so hard-wired to scan for patterns, it's not surprising that we as humans begin to use these patterns to make inferences and tell stories, such as assessing if we are safe or not. "When you find yourself in a situation that's either unfamiliar to you, or not quite familiar enough to get all of your bearings, your natural instinct is to be protective of yourself," Schlozman explains.[2]

As a species, humans have evolved to be self-protective. When we feel threatened now, we can rightly begin to feel anxious and experience physical sensations—our heart speeds up, our stomach drops, and blood floods our extremities. Of course, when a message is unreturned what we are experiencing isn't fear of dying, rather it's felt as *anxiety*. This happens because our brains have evolved tremendously over the past ten thousand years, and the dominant part of our brain, the neocortex, or the advanced mind, plays just as integral a part in creating our anxiety as the ancient survivalist part of the brain. The fear-center (technically referred to as the amygdala and threat center) is responsible for creating self-protective physical responses. In their book *Rewire Your Anxious Brain: How to Use the Neuroscience of Fear to End Anxiety, Panic, and Worry,* authors Catherine M. Pittman and Elizabeth M. Karle make a case that our anxious response is more than fear for our own survival because the brain is vastly interconnected. They state: "Anxiety, it seems, is all around us…[there are] two very different ways that anxiety begins: through what we think about, and through reactions to our environment. This is because anxiety can be initiated by two very different areas of the human brain: the cortex and the amygdala. This understanding is the result of years of research in a field known as neuroscience, which is the science of the structure and function of the nervous system, including the brain."[3]

They argue that "two separate pathways in the brain can give rise to anxiety, and each pathway needs to be understood and treated for maximum relief (Ochsner et al. 2009)."[4] The advanced mind (what they call the "cortex pathway") is, they state, "often a source of anxiety because the frontal lobes anticipate and interpret situations, and anticipation and interpretations often lead to anxiety."[5]

And this anticipation, they assert, "can lead to another common cortex-based process that creates anxiety: worry. Because of our highly developed frontal lobes, humans have the ability to predict future events and imagine their consequences—unlike our pets, who seem to sleep peacefully without anticipating tomorrow's problems. Worry is an outgrowth of anticipation of negative outcomes in a situation. It's a cortex-based process that creates thoughts and images that provoke a great deal of fear and anxiety."[6]

The second pathway leading to anxiety involves the amygdala, or fear-center, which they say "initiates the physical experience of anxiety."[7] They contend that "its strategic location and connections throughout the brain enable it to control the release of hormones and activate areas of the brain that create the physical symptoms of anxiety."[8] And because of this, they assert, "the amygdala exerts powerful and immediate effects on the body."[9] Although the amygdala pathway is, as they say, "very powerful in its ability to activate a variety of physical reactions instantly, anxiety can also have its origins in the cortex pathway."[10] The cortex, or advanced mind, they argue, "operates in a completely different way than the amygdala, but its responses and circuitry can prompt the amygdala to produce anxiety." Through this process, then, they state, "the cortex can create unnecessary anxiety and also worsen anxiety that originates in the amygdala." This is a significant distinction, they claim, because "once you understand how your cortex initiates or contributes to anxiety, you can see the possibilities for either interrupting or modifying cortex reactions to reduce your anxiety."[11]

The authors use an example of a high school senior waiting on a college acceptance letter. He sees a letter, and before opening it, imagines it contains a rejection letter and experiences very anxious moments before opening the envelope. "As it turned out," they write, "he'd been admitted and had even been awarded a scholarship. Nevertheless, his cortex initiated an anxiety response by interpreting the sight of the envelope in a way that created distressing thoughts, and these thoughts activated his amygdala. This type of cortex-based anxiety depends on the cortex's interpretation of the sensory information it receives."[12]

Another way the authors argue the advanced mind works to heighten our anxiety and stress is through a process called *cognitive fusion*, or "believing in the absolute truth of mere thoughts."[13] They write, "Confusing a thought with reality is a very seductive process due to the cortex's tendency to believe it possesses the real meaning of every thought, emotion, or physical sensation. Actually, the cortex is surprisingly prone to misinterpretations and errors. It's common to have erroneous, unrealistic, or illogical thoughts or to experience emotions that don't make much sense. In reality, you need not take every thought or emotion you have seriously. You can allow many thoughts and emotions to simply pass without undue attention or analysis."[14]

When a text isn't returned and you begin to imagine worst-case scenarios or negative things about the person you're communicating with, your mind begins, through the process of cognitive fusion, to believe these things are in fact true—*my boyfriend is definitely cheating, my boss absolutely wants to fire me, my child is dead*—even if you have no evidence to prove these things, you are absolutely convinced of them. Since your advanced mind/neocortex tends to not only create and imagine scenarios but believe they are indeed true, it creates a very real, unnecessary anxious response.

However, the authors state, people often *do* believe what they think, and they tend to ruminate on these thoughts. The authors maintain, "Worry is the process of envisioning negative outcomes for a situation. Rumination is a style of thinking that involves repetitively mulling over problems, relationships, or possible conflicts. In rumination, there's an intense focus on the details and possible causes or effects of situations (Nolen-Hoeksema 2000)."[15] Interestingly, they note, "although people may believe thinking processes like worry or rumination will lead to a solution, what actually happens is a strengthening of the circuitry in the cortex that produces anxiety. In addition, rumination has been shown to lead to depression (Nolen-Hoeksema 2000)."[16]

This ability to ruminate or spiral, Pittman continues, strengthens and reinforces neural circuits to think this way in the future, stating, "Whatever you devote a great deal of time to thinking about or think about in great detail is more likely to be strengthened in your cortex. The circuits in the brain operate on the principle of 'survival of the busiest' (Schwartz and Begley 2003, 17), and whatever circuitry you use repetitively is likely to be very easily activated in the future."[17]

Understanding how the advanced mind and fear center operate together is integral to understanding how the brain becomes hard-wired to behave. The authors state, "instead of leading to solutions, the processes of worry and rumination create deep grooves in your thinking processes that make you tend to focus on these concerns... Sometimes people get lost in repeatedly analyzing situations, creating an experience called anxious apprehension (Engels et al. 2007). As these persistent, worrisome thoughts are rehearsed repeatedly in the mind, they become increasingly difficult to dismiss."[18]

Understanding how our anxiety arises along a theory presented by Ray Kurzweil in *How to Create a Mind,* in which he argues the portion of the brain responsible for the majority of our thoughts is comprised of neural circuits, whose sole function is to identify and categorize patterns. This is vital to understanding why we are "constantly predicting the future and hypothesizing what we will experience."[19]

In other words, our brain is constantly scanning to complete a pattern (find a solution), and the more we do it, the more we reinforce neural pathways and basically train the brain to think a certain way. So now our brains are wired to continually scan the patterns. When patterns aren't complete, we panic. Not because we are fearful of our survival, but because we need some closure, plain and simple. Having our texts and emails go unanswered or answered so ambiguously that the communication loop remains broken—causes us anxiety and stress, not because we fear survival, but simply because that is what the brain does. It goes to the worst-case scenario, because the worst-case scenario is the most final and complete pattern our brain can comprehend.

This hard-wiring kicks in hard when we encounter a broken loop. We'll spend a lot of energy on trying to think of a reason *why* our text remains unanswered because it's just too painful to tolerate the unknown. However, here's where I do agree with Schlozman, who says, "We prefer story to chaos every time." We fill in the blanks of why the interaction has gone awry—typically with a negative development—because we are, in a twisted way, seeking to give ourselves comfort. "Most of us have been let down in the past, making disappointment a familiar sensation. Turning to something familiar—even when it's unpleasant—is in some strange way less painful." It is *less painful*, I would argue, because it's final. It's as final as we can make it. And that is satisfying to our pattern-seeking brain.[20]

What Are We to Do About Dyscommunication Syndrome?

By now you may be wondering, *What's the point in understanding just how painful and how common DCS is? Digital communication isn't going away, so why fixate on how miserable it makes us?*

The simple truth is that an unacknowledged problem can't be addressed. It *is* possible to deal with the stress digital communication can cause, but only *if* you can recognize and understand the stress in the first place and realize how much of the upset has been a party in your head. DCS may be a syndrome, but it doesn't have to be a way of life.

In the next two sections of the book, I'll show you all the subtle and not-so-subtle ways it shows up in all the different areas of your life. You'll learn how to spot the seven stages before you cycle downward, strategies to reduce your suffering when you do inevitably get sucked into a broken loop, as well as tools that will help reduce the number of those incidences in the first place.

But first, in the name of raising your awareness so that you can better see how DCS is affecting you personally, take ten minutes to complete the following self-assessment. Again, you can't change a habit you don't know you have. Also acknowledging the reality of a problem is great motivation for trying to do things differently (something else our brains can resist). As Will Durant so wisely said, "We are what we repeatedly do." And if we're constantly spiraling over unreturned messages, and remain unaware of it, we will continue to do so. And as the stoic philosopher Epictetus wisely remarked centuries ago, "Every habit and capability is confirmed and grows in its corresponding actions, walking by walking, and running by running...therefore, if you want to do something make a habit of it, if [you] don't want to do that, don't, but make a habit of something else instead. The same principle is at work in our state of mind. When you get angry, you've not only experienced that evil, but you've also reinforced a bad habit, adding fuel to the fire."[21]

Self-Assessment Tool #3: How Does Your Mind React to Dyscommunication?

Ask yourself:

- What types of Dyscommunication are most likely to send you into a downward spiral?
- Think of the last time you got profoundly agitated by a broken loop. What were the conditions that preceded it? And then what triggered it? What thoughts did you have while you were in its grips? What did your emotional roller coaster include? Were you annoyed, then angry, then sad, or did you experience a different trajectory of feelings?
- How long did it take you to have your first negative thought?
- What coping mechanisms did you use?
- What actions did you take to close the loop—did you follow up directly with the person? Talk to a friend to get their perspective? Stalk the person on social media? Ultimately damage a relationship?
- Did it resolve itself? How?

- Was it, in the end, about you?
- How are you aware of contributing to the Dyscommunication-related spirals of others?

CHAPTER 4

Dating

"Hi, Andrea. It's me, Peter, from Josh and Nora's wedding."

Peter sets up his first date with Andrea over text. They had met at a mutual friend's wedding, hit it off immediately, and promised to follow up with a coffee. Luckily, he was able to get Andrea's phone number from his friend, the groom.

"Oh! Hi! Peter!" Andrea types back quickly, then almost immediately regretts doing so. *Oh god, he's going to think I am desperate,* Andrea thinks, berating herself. *Why can't you wait a minute, Andrea! Isn't it cool that he had the wherewithal to find out your number and text? Just be cool.*

"Josh passed your number along. Hope you don't mind."

"Not at all, Peter," Andrea says, feeling somewhat giddy.

"So, you still up for coffee? I know a great place on 15th."

"Oh, I know that place! Brewer's Cup! Love it," Andrea replies, throwing caution to the wind and just going for it.

"Great. Can you meet me there tomorrow, say 10 a.m.?"

"Yes! That would be great," Andrea replies quickly.

"Great! See you then! Looking forward to it!" Peter texts back within seconds.

Andrea spends the rest of the day ecstatic. She thinks Peter is so handsome, not to mention smart and a great dancer. And even better, he is good friends with her best friend's new husband. Surely, he has to be a stand-up guy to be friends with Nora and Josh. She resists the urge to text more. Since he was the last one to text, she thought *that clearly meant the ball was in her court to respond and keep the conversation going.* But she decides not to respond. *Don't appear desperate,* Andrea reminds herself, recalling one of the magazine articles she recently read about how not to scare guys away with coming on too strong too soon. *He said they would see each other tomorrow, and that was that,* she assuages herself. But she has a nagging feeling inside… *Should I reply again? I mean…is he expecting me to reply?* Having an open-ended text lingering in her inbox, and not replying to Peter, bothers Andrea all day. *Would he think she wasn't interested?* She just can't wait to get to the coffeehouse the next day. Waiting to know what he is thinking is driving her crazy.

The following day, Peter arrives first at the coffeehouse.

"I'm here," Peter texts quickly. "I got us a table by the window."

Andrea sees the message and is delighted. *He was going through with the date. Phew,* she thinks. For some reason, she had jumped to the worst-case scenario, and had convinced herself that if *she* hadn't replied to him, he might have bailed on her or forgotten all about it.

"On my way! Held up in traffic. Thanks for getting us a spot!" Andrea types back.

"No problem! I'll be here. Take your time," Peter types back.

By all accounts, the date goes great. They share their stories of how they each came to know Josh and Nora. Then they recall some of the highlights of their friends' wedding over the weekend, and move effortlessly on to talking about their mutual love of dogs and binge-watching shows like *Stranger Things*.

At the end of the date, Peter walks Andrea to her car and leans over to kiss her.

Andrea feels butterflies in her stomach. *Could this guy be real? I mean he's basically made for me,* she thinks to herself, but tries to remain calm and not jump the gun. *Be cool, Andrea. Be cool. Get in your car and drive away. Don't say anything stupid.*

Peter smiles and waves as she pulls out of the parking lot and leaves. As Andrea drives away, she berates herself: *Why didn't I say, "We should do this again?" Wait, why didn't he? Would they do this again?* Andrea has no idea. Within minutes her mind begins to spin out. *Oh, god. He hates me. I said something stupid. I must have? Otherwise, wouldn't he have made plans for a follow-up date?*

"Gah!" Andrea shouts in her car. *Why was dating so frustrating? Why couldn't people just say exactly what they meant?* Not knowing how he feels is killing her. Maybe she should text him to say thanks for the great time, but then she thinks she might be coming on too strong if she does so. Nevertheless, to text or not to text lingers over her for the next hour. She texts her friend Nora, who is on her honeymoon, about the date, and inquires whether she should be the first to text Peter back.

"I really like him. I had so much fun on the date," Andrea explains to Nora.

"Then go for it! Just say what you feel. No games!" Nora texts back.

Andrea agrees. She texts Peter right then and there, a solid three hours after the date is over.

"Thanks for the coffee, Peter. I had such a great time."

Over the next few hours, Andrea checks her phone thirty times, but there is no response from Peter.

Why isn't he responding? If he had a good time, he would have reached out by now, Andrea convinces herself. *How could I have been so off base? I'm so stupid! Of course he doesn't like me! He's just like all the others. He's ghosting me. I knew it!*

The following day, Andrea moves from taking things personally to lashing out at Peter. *He probably lied about liking* Stranger Things. *Guys will say anything to get a girl into bed. He probably wanted more than a kiss, and since I drove away and he knew I wasn't going to sleep with him, he moved on to his next prey. So typical!*

By late that evening, Andrea is in full-blown spiral mode. It isn't just Peter who sucks. All men do. And she isn't just going to not have another date with Peter, she is never going to date anyone else, ever again. *I'll be alone for the rest of my life!*

The following day, Andrea considers walking past his office building, just to see if she can spot him. She even fantasizes about going into his office and confronting him about why he didn't write back. Even though Andrea knows she would never actually do that, she can't seem to stop herself from imagining it. She really wants to give him a piece of her mind.

Andrea begins kicking herself. *Why did I get my hopes up again? And why am I so upset that he's not writing back? It's not exactly unusual behavior in this day and age.*

She is still swimming in somber thoughts when a text comes in from Peter later that night, around 9 p.m.

"Hey Andrea! You around?" he asks.

Andrea is relieved, angry, excited, and annoyed all at once. *Should she ask what took him so long? Pretend nothing's wrong? Not bother to answer?* The message she has been pining and hoping for only leaves her more confused and sets her up to spin out all over again.

What in the hell does "You around?" even mean? Andrea wonders. *Does this mean he just wants to have sex?* She is confused and hurt. *Why can't he just say "I had a great time too. I really want to keep seeing you?" Would that be so hard?*

Andrea can't bear the ambiguity or the waiting anymore; she fires off a text and says, "Nice of you to finally reply, Peter! You know I don't think this is going to work out. I don't have time for this drama in my life!"

Peter is stunned. *What?* He thinks to himself. He *just* went out for coffee with her. They didn't sign a marriage certificate. In his mind, they haven't talked for a couple of days—a busy couple of days at work for him. *What drama was she talking about?* he wonders. Of course, he has no idea what has been going on in Andrea's mind over the past two days.

"Ummm, OK. That's too bad, I really enjoyed hanging out with you. Best of luck to you," Peter writes back.

Suddenly, Andrea is overcome with shame. *It's only been two days! What have I done? I blew it because I couldn't just wait for a text. What the hell is wrong with me?*

This common scenario is just one of *many* situations that can cause DCS in dating. In this chapter, we'll explore the many ways Dyscommunication manifests in dating, like it did here for Andrea and Peter. And then, I'll walk you through how to keep the syndrome at bay when it comes to those you date.

When Texting Troubles Cause Dating Dilemmas

Perhaps nothing has introduced as much stress into dating as text messaging. Communication perils in relationships used to be epitomized by waiting at the phone for your crush to call. But back in those dinosaur days, you would, at some point, have to get up and leave the house—and the phone. Now, you have your cellphones in your pocket or your bag, so you're "waiting by the phone" virtually 24/7. And because your crush can just text and doesn't need to have a chunk of free time or be at home or in a quiet place to reach out, it's only natural that you feel like you can expect communication nearly 24/7, too, making DCS an almost sure thing when you don't get a response back.

What's more, in a phone call, each party says what's on their mind without thinking about it too much. But now there's the chance to overthink every bit of your communication: *Should you use an exclamation point? An emoji? How long should you wait to write back?* Not to mention, as I've already covered, texting is ripe for Dyscommunication because there's no tone or body language to help you understand what's being shared.

Here are just some of the triggers that come up in dating relationships, particularly when it comes to texting:

Ghosting:

A day passes without a message from the person you're dating. You send them a quick text making sure all's okay but don't get a reply. A few more days go by. Then a week. Then two weeks. Radio silence. You've been ghosted: they've cut off communication with you without any explanation, vanishing from your life—poof—as if they were never even a part of it in the first place (hence the term).

Talk about being left in limbo. Did something happen to them? Are they still alive? Were you that horrible to be around? Are they just an asshole? Are they currently on a beach in Mexico getting married?

With the communication loop not just broken, but completely severed, by the other person, and with no explanation as to why, ghosting is Dyscommunication on steroids, and thus the perfect trigger for a maelstrom of DCS.

The cycle starts with anxiety about the silence, and then you try to complete the broken loop with negative thoughts: You take it personally and think you must have done something to run them off, that there must be something wrong with you. And then you're tempted to send a bunch of angry texts saying how dare they do this to you, on and on down the spiral.

Ghosting is rejection times two: not only don't they want to continue dating you, they don't even want to give you a reason. For these reasons, and because it's not likely you'll get closure anytime soon, if ever, it's no wonder that studies show that intense social rejection—such as being ghosted suddenly by someone you have romantic feelings for—activates the same pathways in the brain as actual physical pain.[1] (There is some good news in this: acetaminophen has been shown in multiple studies to reduce the emotional and physical pain of social rejection[2,3]—hey, it can't hurt.)

First off, know this: You're not alone. According to the most oft-quoted ghosting statistic, nearly 80 percent of single and dating people between the ages of eighteen and thirty-three have been ghosted at least once.[4] That survey was conducted in 2016, and it showed a dramatic increase from a 2014 poll by the Huffington Post and data company YouGov, which suggested only 18 percent of millennials had been ghosted by someone they were dating.[5] It stands to reason that today the numbers could very well be higher, even much higher, than 80 percent. (Interestingly, ghosting may actually be occurring just as frequently in the business world: According to a 2019 poll by job-posting website Indeed.com, about 83 percent of companies surveyed who were recruiting new hires said they'd been ghosted by potential candidates.)[6]

Unfortunately, part of the pain of ghosting is that it's highly unpredictable. You can get ghosted after one date or two, or after months of dating, and the intensity of the rejection typically climbs the longer the relationship.

Why do people behave so ghoulishly? Although the paranormal-inspired phenomenon has only been labeled as such in recent years (it was first reported on as a term by the *New*

York Times, which defined it as "the ultimate silent treatment," in 2015),[7] people have certainly long ignored or avoided one another, so psychologists do have some idea why ghosting happens. Plus, more research into modern dating via apps has revealed insight into behaviors like ghosting as well. So, what are some of the reasons experts suggest your date might ghost you?

- **Technology seemingly gives them permission.** Dating apps can dehumanize the whole dating process, making it easier for someone to throw common courtesy and empathy out the window. What's more, apps allow us to meet people we might otherwise never meet: total strangers who aren't friends of friends or acquaintances of family members or coworkers. In other words, because they have no other connection to you outside of the app, they may feel they can ghost without any real consequences.

- **They want to avoid conflict.** Ghosting says an awful lot about how someone deals with their emotions and confrontation. Namely, that they don't. We can all want to or wish we could avoid things that make us uncomfortable but doing so shows a lack of emotional maturity.

- **They have strong destiny beliefs.** A 2018 study divided participants into two groups: one that believes that relationships are fated to work out (or not) and another that believes that relationships take work to grow. The people who believe in the idea of destiny were 60 percent more likely to ghost. They have a strong belief in finding "the one," and when they decide you may not be it, for whatever reason, they don't feel the need to put in effort.[8]

- **They don't want to hurt you.** Ironically, a ghoster may think they're doing you a favor by vanishing. (Clearly, they haven't yet heard of DCS!) They don't want to hurt your feelings by saying they're not interested, so they say nothing at all. Of course, this ties into how they deal with conflict and attachment for that matter, too: avoidance.

- **Their behavior is more noticeable now.** People have been ignoring each other for eons; it's just that now that we have so very many ways to communicate with people, not connecting is glaringly obvious.

- **It's sort of an accident.** I know it seems like *the* most deliberate thing a person you're dating could do, but think back to the information I've shared about how many texts, not to mention emails and calls, we get in a day. If the person you're casually dating is also casually dating or talking with other people, some correspondence is just bound to fall through the cracks.

Notice something about all these reasons? None of them have anything to do with something being wrong with you or with you doing anything wrong! Remember, 90 percent of the time Dyscommunication is not your fault, and is a needless exercise in self-inflicted misery.

So, what can you do to keep DCS from setting in if you get ghosted?

1. **Try once more.** After two days of not hearing from someone, it's perfectly acceptable to follow up. We are all getting so many texts all the time that it is inevitable that we miss one or two here and there or that we see it and want to respond thoughtfully, but then the influx of new emails and texts pushes it out of our minds. So, reach out again with a specific yet low-stakes ask, such as "Hey, I've been trying to connect with you, when is a good time for us to talk?" Not something vague, like "Hey, I'm trying again" or even "What's up?" If you don't hear a response to this second communication, there's your answer. Resist the urge to also send an email and leave a voicemail and message them on Instagram—if they're avoiding you in one medium, they're avoiding you in all of them, and the barrage of communications will only make you look impatient at best and like a stalker at worst.

2. **Remind yourself it's not about you.** Again and again, as many times as it takes. If it gets really bad—and you're experiencing physical pain over the loss—ask a trusted friend to remind you whenever you need it that it. is. not. your. fault.

3. **After your second try, don't reach out.** If you've tried the one specific yet polite follow-up and haven't heard back, the overwhelming odds are that you're being ghosted. So, really, don't keep pinging them—and don't obsessively check their social media accounts either. Doing so will only perpetuate the DCS cycle. Completely ending all contact is the best way to get over your ghost and stay

sane in the process. Remember how I alluded to closure earlier? While you may not get the *why* you want from a ghost, after your follow-up attempt goes unanswered, their behavior is closure. Try closing the loop by telling yourself that they have made their choice, for whatever reason (that doesn't have to do with you) and move on.

4. **Seek support.** While I'm not aware of any ghosting support groups, with statistics what they are, you're guaranteed to know someone who's gone through it. Talk about it when you need to.

Tempted to ghost someone yourself? Remember how you felt when it happened to you and defy the desire to Dyscommunicate. It really isn't an appropriate way to end a romantic relationship, whether one that's completely new or one that's gone on for a while. (However, if you're in one of those abusive or seriously toxic relationships in which your life is in danger, and you need to get away without risking personal injury, then by all means— ghost.) If you're not in danger, talk openly and honestly with the person you're dating and explain why you want to call things off instead. Do so in a text only if you must—but even this substandard mode of communication is preferable to simply cutting off all contact. You know the spiral being ghosted initiates; having that knowledge and choosing to do it anyway goes beyond DCS and veers into that even darker territory of passive-aggression and manipulation. Take a stand for closing the loop, even when the outcome of that closure is the end of a relationship.

Dick Pics:

There's not a lot of ambiguity when it comes to the meaning behind a dick pic…or is there? A woman is trying to communicate with the man she's dating, whether casually or seriously: maybe she texts to ask about future plans or to express her emotions for him. First, there's a delay in response—the Dyscommunication begins. And then, boom: A dick pic pops up on the screen. How does it close the loop her text opened? It doesn't. Sure, it communicates that he's got sex on his mind (hopefully sex with her), but it doesn't tell her anything beyond that. It's an entirely unsatisfactory response that leaves things just as unresolved as no response or a response that only half addresses the original message. Thus, it can easily trigger DCS and start the spiral of negative thoughts. She takes it personally, then moves into the stage of distrust, thinking: *He doesn't take me seriously. He doesn't really like me and is only interested in me sexually.*

What you do with a dick pic is up to you. You can try again to get your original text answered or otherwise responded to. Or, of course, you can take it as a signal that this person may not be the best communicator or the right person for you. Unless, of course, you're strictly interested in a physical relationship and don't care about dialogue. In which case, hey, this might be the man of your dreams! (Or at least the man of tonight.)

All that being said, if you haven't even met this person in person yet (because you met on an online dating app) and one of his first messages is a dick pic, you don't owe him any response. It's like Maya Angelou proclaimed, "When someone shows you who they are, believe them the first time." He's a poor, aggressive communicator. You have full permission to ghost! No explanation needed. He only needs to look through his texts to see the reason why you didn't respond if the last pic is one of his dick.

The Booty Call:

Texting has also opened the door to a dissolution in the concept of the traditional date, where you plan to spend time together on a certain day at a certain time. Now, it's much more common to get a noncommittal text, which is usually a booty call—aka an invitation for casual sex—late in the evening, as Andrea did in the story that opened this chapter. Even if the late-night, last-minute text is truly an ask for some version of a date and not just a hookup, it's still problematic because it makes getting together more a matter of convenience than a true desire to spend time with someone. It's kind of like the channel surfing of old—turning on the television to see what's on, or in this case, who's available. It's not the desire to spend time with you as an individual that's driving it so much as it's a need for distraction in human form.

It's easy to see how a booty call can start the spin of DCS. To begin with, you've likely waited all day—or multiple days—for some kind of communication. When it does come, it's usually vague and thus easily misunderstood. Think again about Andrea's story: Can she be sure it's a booty call? Or could he possibly be reaching out so that he can explain why he took so long to text her back? If just that one text pops up or, worse, that one text with three dots and another message that never comes, she'll be well down the downward spiral in no time.

Much like a dick pic, how you respond to the booty call is, well, your call. You can share your frustration and anxiety about the original delayed response and seek to get your original text answered or otherwise responded to. Or you can move on if you're wanting more out of the relationship. Whatever you do, just don't ghost!

The Roadblock to Intimacy

When you're dating, texting can give a false sense of relationship. People often text when they're bored or to avoid loneliness. It may not be because they have a genuine interest in getting to know you better and cultivating a meaningful relationship. It doesn't take much investment of time to keep a text string going for a few hours or even a few days, and even the wittiest banter in text form is not equal to true interest, caring, or connection. It's also just impossible to get a true read on someone based on their electronic communications, no matter how responsive. No text string can make up for meeting in person and experiencing the level of attraction, interest, and safety you feel in the presence of that person. It certainly takes more time out of your schedule to meet in person than to fire off a text, but if you're looking for something more than a distraction, it can only save you time over the long run to use some of that initial texting to schedule a time to meet up.

Think about it: When you see a person's body language and hear the intonation in their voice, you get emotional feedback. Not so with texting. There are more opportunities than ever to misread the other person's intent.

You can text while you're doing a million other things. It isn't mindful communication; without that connection to your own awareness, there's no emotional intimacy. While not everything you say to your potential partner has to be deep and meaningful—sometimes you just need to tell them you're running ten minutes late, after all—having vulnerable conversations is vital to building and maintaining romantic relationships. Texting can provide a simulation of vulnerability, but it's a cheap substitute for having intimate conversations in person.

What You Can Do About It

The steps and tips that I'll outline in Chapter 9 are a good place to start to solve DCS in any type of relationship. Admittedly, some of them can be harder to do in new dating relationships than others. After all, unless you start dating a longtime friend, dating involves communicating with someone who is essentially a stranger. When you don't know someone, it can be more difficult to stay in the present moment and look at the facts or look for positive explanations about why they may not be texting back. After all, you don't yet know their routines and what their day might really be like. You're already in fear because it's new! You want them to like you, and you're fearful they won't.

Here's a radical idea to avoid DCS if you're just starting to date someone: Take texting off the table. Seriously. I know of a couple who went this route early on in their relationship and to great results. A few dates into their relationship, Rachel dealt with an all-consuming family emergency. She was getting texts from the man, Jack, that were full of excitement for their next date and requests to make plans. In the middle of the whirlwind with her family, she simply texted that she'd write back soon. And then she forgot. The Dyscommunication spiral started for Jack, until eventually he reached out and asked if she was okay and explained he was hurt to not hear from her. Emotional and exhausted from her personal difficulties, Rachel felt so overwhelmed by the message that she decided to just call things off all together. With what was happening with her family, now just wasn't a good time to date, she told herself.

Eventually, things settled down and Rachel realized she *did* want to date Jack. Thankfully, he said yes to another meetup, and it was then and there they decided not to text—at least not all day every day as their primary communication and method of getting to know each other. They both had big things going on at work and needed to focus on their projects without any chance of succumbing to the maelstrom of DCS. And they didn't want it to come in between them…again. So, they made plans for the next date before each date was through and only used texting for short, logistical messages such as to say *I'm running 10 minutes late.* They found they had so much to talk about when they did see each other in person, and they were more excited, not to mention calmer, at their meetings. After all, there were no open loops leading up to them. Refreshing, right?

If it sounds too scary to almost eliminate texting from your dating relationship, I get it. You don't have to do as Rachel and Jack did. Perhaps you'd prefer to be able to text good morning and good night or to be able to send a few sweet notes to one another here and there. That's okay, too. The goal is just to avoid either one of you opening a loop that might not get closed.

▌ Tips for Dating to Avoid Dyscommunication

- **Talk about it.** It's important for romantic partners to have a conversation about how they prefer to stay in contact and how quickly they expect each other to respond to each communication—a step most people never take and one that can go a surprisingly long way toward alleviating DCS. This is communicating your needs, after all! Do you need and want a few check-ins throughout the day? Would you prefer email over text, or maybe just one call at lunchtime? If the other person is busy and can't send a long response, do you want them to at least quickly share it's not a good time? You and your partner set the rules. And then when you abide by them, loops aren't opened, and Dyscommunication can be avoided.

- **Check the clock.** Even if you have laid down some rules for texting and otherwise communicating with your partner, always remain mindful of when you're messaging. If you've written a long, complicated message that requires a long, complicated response, maybe wait to send it until after your partner is off work, for example. With its immediacy, texting can make us feel that we need to be as on-call in our relationships as we feel tethered to work with emails 24/7. When you feel the urge to text your partner, just check in with yourself first to see if it's a feasible time for them to be able to respond. If you aren't sure, sending a quick "Do you have a minute?" or "Can you chat?" text will help respect their time and their other obligations.

- **Take texts at face value.** I know it can be difficult to do, but challenge yourself to read each text just for what it is and to respond appropriately. Don't imagine a tone of voice that may or may not be there. What are the facts given to you in that message? In a way, this is practicing mindfulness. You're staying in the present moment, trying not to read, well, subtext into a text based on anything from your past or any worry about the future.
- **Remind yourself it's not you, it's them.** Remember, if you've gotten no response, *it almost never has anything to do with you.*
- **Pick up the phone.** Unless you've been ghosted and you're trying to move on, if you truly can't stop the worry and anxiety and need to close the loop, call your partner and/or ask to meet face-to-face. Try to get the answer and communication you need. Taking another tip to heart, though: maybe shoot a quick text and ask if it's an okay time to call. If they don't pick up, you don't want the spiral to begin all over again.

Self-Assessment Tool #4: How Much Is My Dating Life Being Affected by Dyscommunication?

Do you:

1) Get anxious when you haven't heard from someone you're texting?
2) Become irritable when waiting for a reply?

3) Catastrophize and create elaborate narratives of why someone isn't getting back to you?

4) Spend a lot of time trying to "interpret" texts from others, i.e., discuss them with friends and loved ones, and are unable to accept them at face value?

5) Find yourself unable to talk yourself down and feel regretful after sending a nasty text message?

6) Ever ghost people or feel there is a legitimate reason not to respond to someone else?

7) Ruin potential relationships before they start because of text messaging?

CHAPTER 5

Relationships

Henry was always the perfect son. He was smart, gregarious, good-looking—with steel-blue eyes and a face that often was mistaken for the Hollywood star Zac Efron. His parents, Jen and Greg, adored him, as did his little sister, Karen (15), and brother, Oliver (13). They looked up to their older brother and hung on his every word. A straight-A honors student and star varsity track-and-field all-star, Henry had a bright and promising future ahead of him. He and his girlfriend of three years, Annie, both got into the colleges of their dreams and were even their high school's prom king and queen. Nothing seemed to be getting in their way.

Everybody at their high school thought Henry and Annie made the perfect couple, too. He was sweet, handsome, and sensitive. Popular, but approachable, Annie was the envy of all the girls in her class (and the first crush of most of the guys). Nominated for the yearbook's "Friendliest" and "Nicest Smile" superlatives, Annie never met a person who didn't fall instantly in love with her beauty, charm, and kindness. She too was excited to start college in the fall. She was accepted to her state's university and into their prestigious pre-med program. She hoped to one day become a pediatrician and take over her father's family practice. She and Henry had their whole life planned—she would become a doctor, and he, a lawyer. They would have two kids and settle down in the same town they grew up in—and have their beloved families nearby. Nothing seemed to be holding these two lovebirds back. Not even the potential of a long-distance love.

However, as fall approached, something unraveled in Henry as he began thinking about attending a different college than Annie. There were just so many unknowns. Just the thought of it all made him sick. He couldn't handle it. It wasn't long before he began to fear the worst, and he became increasingly convinced that Annie was going to break up with him and begin dating someone new as soon as she went away to college. He expressed as much to his mom and dad over dinner one night in August before Annie was to leave, and his parents (and his siblings) assured him that Annie loved him and there was nothing to worry about.

"You two nerds will be so busy with all your schoolwork and sports, you won't have time to date anyone else!" Henry's dad joked.

But Henry couldn't hear his father's joke; he was busy checking his phone throughout the dinner and was distracted. He had texted Annie earlier in the evening and hadn't heard back from her.

"Maybe put the phone away, Henry?" his mom, Jen, suggested. "You know she is working at the country club right now. Just enjoy your dinner. Come on. You know the rules—*no phones at dinner!*"

Henry grew agitated and threw the phone down. "Fine, Mom! God!"

Jen could see that her son was obviously upset and advised that maybe he should limit the text messages. As a mother, she felt like it was all she was doing these days—constantly having this same conversation now with all three of her teenage children. If it wasn't Henry on the phone with his girlfriend texting her all hours of the day and night, it was her two younger teenagers, constantly updating and refreshing their social media pages and texting their friends endlessly. And in between all the texting was the drama and upset that came from the content (or lack thereof) of the texts themselves. It was amazing she could ever get her own job done, let alone speak to her children, with all the text-drama going on each day in her house. She was starting to lose control of her children—and her family. She was so uneasy about the phones, she often wished she could just get rid of them, but she knew they needed them. For one thing, it was how she kept tabs on all her kids. It was nearly impossible to reach them any other way than text. She could barely get them to focus on a live conversation with her. Besides, it seemed it would be social suicide to keep her children from social media and texting. It was the only way these kids seemed to talk these days.

However, Jen could sense something wasn't quite right with her oldest son. He had been increasingly agitated as the summer went on. She could sense that as the day came closer for Annie to leave for college, Henry was even more connected to his phone.

She also noticed he was completely disengaging with the family. He would barely come out of his room. When he wasn't out with Annie, he was texting her constantly. He seemed obsessed with Annie's every move, and he was constantly checking to see if she had responded to his latest text. Jen was concerned.

Annie was dealing with the upcoming separation much differently than her boyfriend. She had thrown herself into her summer job and was having fun making new friends at the country club restaurant where she was waiting tables. She loved to keep busy. She also loved meeting new people and hanging out with them in person. She didn't share Henry's fears or insecurities. She loved Henry. There was never a doubt in her mind they would make it. She knew that the separation would be hard on their relationship, but she believed with all her heart that they would make long-distance work. Besides, they had their phones! It was like they were tethered together 24/7 already, she thought. Not a minute went by when either of them wasn't texting each other, even over the most mundane details or memes and TikToks they shared throughout the day.

"Did you see this?" Henry asked.

"Yep." Annie replied. "HAHA. So funny."

"I have to run to the store for my mom. Will you still be working?"

"Yes."

"What time do you get off? Usual? 10?" Henry asked.

"No. I am closing tonight, so 11."

"Wanna hangout after?"

"Can't tonight. So tired. Have the early shift tomorrow," Annie replied.

This was typical fare. Their conversations would go on throughout the day and night, like they had for the past three years. They talked about everything and nothing. They fought on text. They made up on text. Sometimes they texted hundreds of texts in a single day. It was like an ongoing conversation that only ended when they were both asleep.

But this last text thread was different. It wasn't like Annie to say no to seeing him. Henry always stopped by her work and said hi or walked her to her car after a shift. And sometimes they would go back to her place for a while. He felt something was off. Annie had been hanging out with other waiters at the country club all summer. One of them, Ben, was going to the same college as Annie in the fall. Every time Annie mentioned Ben's name to Henry, his stomach fell. Henry had met Ben back in June and immediately hated him. Ben was handsome, smart, and funny. Henry was convinced Annie had a crush on him. And worst of all, Ben was basically around Annie eight hours a day now—time Henry didn't get with his girlfriend.

Henry's mind went to some dark places immediately after receiving the text from Annie. As soon as Annie said she didn't want to meet up with him, he imagined that she was going to hang out with Ben instead. Though Annie had never lied to Henry before, he couldn't help but feel like Annie *was lying now.* He was utterly convinced she was.

"Is Ben working with you?" Henry texted back.

"Yeah," Annie said.

Henry became enraged. *Some other guy is hanging out with my girlfriend.*

"You are going out with him after?" Henry asked.

"What?" Annie asked.

"ARE YOU GOING OUT WITH BEN AFTER WORK?" Henry wrote in all caps, letting her know just how angry he was.

"I'm not doing this," Annie typed back. She didn't have time to talk Henry down during one of his moods. She was at work, and her manager would dock her tips if he caught her texting while waiting on customers.

On the other end, Henry looked at the words. *"I'm not doing this…"* and thought and thought about what those words meant. *That was ambiguous. What wasn't she doing? The relationship anymore?* Henry was incensed.

Henry texted her back.

"Are you breaking up with me?"

No reply. Minutes went by and Henry began typing "Are you fucking Ben? Is this what it's all about?"

Again, no reply from Annie. Henry's mind was reeling.

"So, are you going to wait to leave for college and then dump me, so you and Ben are free to screw around, so you don't have to do it behind my back anymore?" Henry typed angrily.

Over the course of the next several hours, Annie had no idea these texts were coming in. After Henry's last upsetting text, she had turned her phone's silent mode on and slipped it in her pocket so she could try to stay focused on her job.

I'll just talk to him when I get home. I am exhausted, she had thought when she turned off her phone, having no idea what was going on in Henry's mind or what he was typing.

After her shift ended, she and her coworker Ben pulled all the ketchup bottles from the tables to marry them and to roll silverware in preparation for the next day. They were both assigned to close, so that meant they also had to put up all the chairs, sweep, mop, and then lock up the restaurant together. Ben and Annie worked quickly side by side with each other. They were too tired to talk much, and both were eager to be done as quickly as possible and get home. Annie thought Ben was nice, but too quiet for her liking. She wished she had someone to talk to make the time pass quicker.

Meanwhile, Henry had worked himself into a full-blown rage. *Annie was doing this on purpose. She was ignoring him. She was probably with Ben right now. Lying bitch!* Henry couldn't handle the thought of Annie hanging out with another man. He imagined Ben taking off Annie's clothes in the storeroom of the restaurant. Then he imagined them having sex. Quickly, the thoughts escalated to various revenge fantasies. He imagined killing Ben. Then it occurred to Henry, almost as if it made total sense, that killing Ben was *exactly* what needed to happen. Ben was the problem. Clearly. In that moment, Henry ran to his father's bedroom closet and pulled down his father's handgun that he kept high on a shelf in the corner. He knew his father never locked the gun because he kept the bullets in another room. Henry walked down the hall to his father's den, opened the top desk drawer where he knew his dad stored the bullets. Without a second thought, he grabbed the bullets, dropped them in the gun's chamber, put the gun in his pocket, and calmly walked down the stairs—finally feeling for the first time in weeks like he knew exactly what he needed to do to end this constant feeling of anxiety whirling within him.

"Where are you going, Henry?" his mom called out from the living room, where she was watching a movie with the rest of the family, who were all sitting on the couch with their own devices, barely paying attention to the large screen in front of them.

"Going to meet up with Annie after her shift," Henry called out.

"Okay. Tell her hello for us!" Jen called back, never looking up from her phone to see just how agitated her son looked.

"Drive safe!" Henry's dad, Greg, yelled after him, not looking up from his phone either.

Henry said nothing and slammed the door behind him, running toward his car. He was on a mission.

While driving, he pulled his phone out and saw that Annie still hadn't responded. *God! How hard is it to just respond, Annie!* He threw the phone on the passenger side seat. *Fuck you. And fuck Ben too.*

As he was driving, he saw a text come on the phone on the seat beside him. All he saw in the sample window of the incoming text were the words: "This is Ben…I am with Annie…"

He didn't even bother opening the text or looking. He was enraged now. *"That asshole is dead…."* Henry pushed his foot hard on the accelerator and his car sped toward the country club.

Unbeknownst to Henry, back at the restaurant, just as Ben and Annie were about to lock up, Annie looked at her phone for the first time in hours. She had forgotten that she turned off the notifications. When she opened Henry's messages, she was shocked at what she saw. She began to shake as she read dozens of texts from Henry accusing her of all sorts of awful things. She could barely believe what she was reading. She hardly recognized her boyfriend. She began to cry. Ben asked her what the matter was and asked to see her phone. She handed it over. She was still shaking.

"I don't know why he is saying all of this!" Annie cried.

"Don't worry, I'll just text him and tell him we're just co-workers and that I have a girlfriend and there is nothing to worry about. I know this sounds crazy, but I read somewhere men will be much more likely to believe other men than their own girlfriends," Ben said, shaking his head, as if he couldn't believe he had to do such a thing, as he texted Henry on Annie's behalf.

"This is Ben…I am with Annie…she is really upset and can't type right now. She wants me to let you know that absolutely nothing is going on between us. We are just coworkers. I have a girlfriend. I'd be happy to talk to you myself and answer any questions you have. We can all sort this out together. Just calm down, Bro. She loves you."

Annie thanked Ben. Then Ben reached out to hug her and console her.

"It's all right, Annie. I know you're not asking my opinion, but if you ask me, you deserve better than a paranoid boyfriend. Just sayin'. I would never talk to my girlfriend this way. He seems kind of unstable right now. I would just be careful."

Annie began to sob, and Ben held her tighter.

Just then, Annie heard footsteps coming up the walkway behind Ben. From out of the shadows, she saw Henry step forward out into the light and point the gun at Ben's back.

Annie tried to pull away from Ben. "No, Henry! It's not what it looks like! NO!"

She heard the gunshot and then suddenly felt the weight of Ben's body fall toward her. "Stop, Henry! Ohmygod! What are you doing!" Annie yelled as she bent over Ben, trying to stop the bleeding. "Oh Ben! Ben! No!"

Henry couldn't take hearing Annie say Ben's name anymore. He walked quickly over to Ben's body and then aimed the gun at the head of his beloved girlfriend, who was leaning over Ben and trying to help him, all the while crying out Ben's name over and over. Henry couldn't take it anymore. He had so convinced himself that Annie and Ben were a couple, that her saying his name was just further evidence of it. Without another thought, Henry pulled the trigger and shot Annie. Annie went silent. She slumped over and collapsed onto her coworker Ben.

Henry didn't linger. He ran back to his car. His heart was racing. But before he could pull away, he saw his phone had a message alert. He opened the message, and this time he read the message all the way through...*"Just calm down, Bro. She loves you."*

Henry's hands were the ones shaking now. He couldn't believe what he had just done. It was as if he had just awoken from an intense nightmare. He felt so ashamed. *He had killed his girlfriend, the love of his life.* He had ruined her life, her family's life. He had ruined his too, not to mention his mom and dad and siblings, who loved him so much. He also ruined a stranger's life—and his family's and his girlfriend's lives too. Deeply remorseful, Henry began sobbing. He felt he knew what he had to do. There didn't seem to be any other choice. He pulled out his phone. He looked up his contacts and found his Family thread—his mom, dad, sister Karen, and brother Oliver's numbers, and then looked up Annie's parents' numbers. Then he simply typed the words:

"I am so, so sorry, everyone. I hope someday you can all forgive me. I love you. Bye."

Henry put down his phone for a final time. He then took the gun out of his pocket, held it to his head, and used the last of his father's bullets on himself.

The tragic story of Henry, Annie, and Ben, while rare and an extreme case of what happens when DCS goes unchecked, is nevertheless a real and present threat. Murder-suicides in the U.S. are not as uncommon as you might think among teens, and real events that I weaved into this story happen all over the world every day. Outside of unintentional injuries, which account for half of all U.S. teen deaths, homicide and suicide are the other leading killers of teenagers. The purpose of this story, however, is not to illustrate murder-suicide among teenagers, but rather the various stages of DCS in clear and present detail in this extreme but likely case:

1. <u>Anxiety and agitation</u>

For weeks, Henry's facing the unknown (ending high school, starting college, and beginning a long-distance relationship with his longtime girlfriend) put his body and mind in high alert. There were so many unknowns up ahead, his pattern-seeking advanced mind was working in overdrive trying to fix his broken loops by picking the worst-case scenarios to help assuage his anxious mind. When he sent texts and got an ambiguous reply from Annie ("I am not doing this") and then heard nothing for several hours, his mind literally couldn't handle the open-endedness of the conversation.

2. Taking it personally

Henry immediately took the lack of response from Annie personally. Instead of thinking rationally—that Annie was busy working and didn't have time to write lengthy explanations as to why she couldn't meet up with him after—he believed she was purposefully being ambiguous, avoiding him, and trying to screw with his mind.

3. Resentment and distrust

This led him to accuse Annie of lying. Instead of taking her text at face-value—that she was closing at work, was tired, and wanted to just go home and rest because she had a long work-day ahead of her—Henry accused Annie of lying. He believed without a shadow of a doubt that she had other plans, and there was nothing to convince him otherwise.

4. Catastrophizing

This is where Henry's DCS escalates and goes off the proverbial rails. It is also a case that fully illustrates both the dangers and full extent of catastrophizing. A smart boy with a clever and active imagination, Henry's advanced mind goes into overdrive here. He's not just adept at creating worst-case scenarios (i.e., *she is going to break up with me*), he's practically writing complete novels in his own mind. His advanced mind/neocortex is busy all night drafting and narrating epic-level dramas that are sending messages to his fear-center and ramping up his sense of anxiety and dread. His jealousy of Ben, Annie's coworker, reaches a fever pitch when Henry imagines his girlfriend having sex with Ben. Henry's mind creates a vivid image—and it is so clear—it feels real to him. What is happening here is a cognitive (thinking) process, as you recall the authors of *Rewire Your Anxious Mind* referred to it as *cognitive fusion* or "believing in the absolute truth of mere thoughts."[1] Henry was, as the authors write, "Confusing a thought with reality."[2] This, they add, "is a very seductive process due to the cortex's tendency to believe it possesses the real meaning of every thought, emotion, or physical sensation. The cortex is surprisingly prone to misinterpretations and errors. It's common to have erroneous, unrealistic, or illogical thoughts or to experience emotions that don't make much sense."[3] In other words, it feels very much to Henry that all the things he is thinking *are* actually taking place—even though they are completely erroneous and false. He then uses his advanced mind to imagine killing Ben. And this is also satisfying. Even if it's murder—killing your girlfriend's supposed lover feels better than the unknown. What could be more satisfying an ending and completion of a broken loop than that!

5.   Possibly doing something you regret

Not only does Henry begin sending all sorts of vicious texts to his girlfriend, he also begins taking steps to follow through on his revenge fantasy. Swept up in the whirlwind of wanting to kill Ben—and convincing himself it is the only reasonable solution to his problems—Henry has stepped in the realm of doing things he will most certainly regret. He steals his father's gun and bullets.

6.   Inability to talk yourself down

Henry can't even talk himself down at this point. Everything he sees or hears now is just more evidence that Annie is cheating. The text he doesn't bother opening and reading in full is a classic case of Dyscommunication as well. If he had just calmed down, opened the text and read it, he would have seen that Annie wasn't cheating and that Ben was not a threat. However, given his state of mind at this point, it is possible that even if he had read the complete message, he wouldn't have believed Ben. Henry couldn't talk himself down.

7. Feeling ashamed

It wasn't until he was back in his car that Henry realized the magnitude of what he had done. Pulling a trigger on a gun multiple times is a sobering experience. Watching someone he loved die in front of him at his own hands certainly jolted him out of his haze of delusion. It suddenly became very clear to him that what he did was wrong. When he finally opened the text from Ben and read it all the way through, he realized Ben was right. *Annie did love him.* He had overreacted. He let his catastrophic thinking get out of hand. He felt so ashamed and was so full of regret, he felt he had no choice but to kill himself.

Henry's case points out three key things:

1) **Catastrophizing is more than dreaming up just a worst-case scenario.** It's a full-blown cognitive process that involves the advanced mind's full support and collaboration. Henry was adept at storytelling and narration. In his mind he had created all sorts of scenarios that became more vivid and felt more real the more he thought about them. Catastrophizing is the delusional, crazy-making process that goes on in our minds when our minds can't complete a pattern. It's an endless search

for an end to the broken loop through storytelling. Henry had convinced himself that his sweet, kind, and loving girlfriend was lying, cheating, and purposefully trying to hurt him by not responding. And nothing could have been further from the truth.

2) **Another key aspect that triggers DCS is the ambiguity of texts as well as not reading them all the way through.** It's impossible to read a person's mind or understand what is really going in someone's experience. Henry had no way of knowing just how busy Annie was at work. He had no idea what her frame of mind was. He was operating from his own point of view and took it all personally. Similarly, not reading the entire text or email can also invite Dyscommunication. Henry failed to read the entire text from Ben. He read the first two lines and his mind immediately thought the worst. Reading a text or email in full and taking a few minutes to process the information might have, in this case, saved lives.

3) **It was clear that one of the problems here was one of extreme usage and dependence on text messages alone to carry on conversations.** Henry's mom alluded to it, but she couldn't quite name the problem at the time. She had a feeling her son was spending far too much time texting and waiting on texts, and not enough time engaged in real life and real conversations. She herself recognized that everyone in the family was hooked on their devices, and she even admitted that she was too—if she didn't converse with them over text,

it just wasn't happening. Sherry Turkle, founder and director of the MIT Initiative on Technology and Self, writes in her book *Alone Together* that in her studies, kids reported that their parents were addicted to their devices, and they wished the adults would put down their screens and pay more attention to their kids. For better or worse, our kids see us perpetually engaging with electronic communications that they can see cause us stress and anxiety. An observational study of caregivers eating in a fast-food restaurant with children found that when caregivers are using a mobile device, there are fewer interactions with the children—both verbal and nonverbal.[4]

Like it or not, phones aren't going anywhere, and they have become an integral part of how couples (adults and teens alike) communicate—and yes—Dyscommunicate. The average American child gets their first smartphone at the age of 10.3, down from twelve years old in 2012.[5] It's no wonder, then, that as soon as they get their own devices, kids use them to an even greater extent—as an example, teens receive an average of 124 texts per day, compared to seventy-five for adults. Most parents give their kids smartphones so that they'll always be able to reach them; it's a safety thing, just as Jen mentioned in the story above. And then, of course, the phone becomes the primary way your kids stay in touch with friends. They are constantly texting and chatting with friends in apps, instantly responding to each other at all hours of the day and night—even when they're in the same room together. (Except when you text them; then, there's an interminable delay before you hear back!) And when you spend time together as a family, they are more than likely to be immersed in their phones with their friends, girlfriends, or boyfriends. The safety tool becomes a tool of disconnect between people—and ultimately affects everyone around as well as the couple. But there are ways to mitigate this.

▋ Tips for Relationships to Avoid DCS

- **Establishing screen-free zones and times.** Whether it's a room in the house, the car, or a certain time of day, such as the dinner hour, there have to be designated areas and times for couples to unplug from their devices and talk face-to-face. Being tethered to a phone all day and making it the primary source of communication in any relationship is unhealthy. Teens should not sleep next to their phones. (Adults shouldn't either.) According to a 2019 study "The New Normal: Parents, Teens, Screens, and Sleep in the United States" done by consumer advocacy group Common Sense, four out of five teenagers with mobile devices keep them in their rooms overnight—and nearly a third of those bring them into their beds while sleeping. The survey also found that sleeping with phones "undermine[s] cognitive functioning" and was the key source of conflict within homes, and that many parents feared the devices were causing their teens to become "addicted." The survey showed that teens use their phones "round-the-clock" and reported using them right before bedtime and immediately upon rising, and some reported getting up in the middle of the night to check their phone.[6] However, the study also showed that the apple didn't fall far from the tree, and most adults admitted to the same behavior. Research shows that when people (teens and adults alike) sleep next to their devices, they don't sleep as well and feel the need to constantly be checking their devices, further impacting their mental health and making them prone to anxiety.

- **Prioritize opportunities to connect face-to-face**. Meals are a perfect time for connecting face-to-face. When watching movies together, playing board games, or sitting together outside, also make it clear that the priority is face-to-face conversation and that phones should be kept away. Plan events such as hikes, bike rides, or other outings that encourage conversation, and make it impossible to check one's phone.

- **Ask yourself what is really upsetting you**. Get to the heart of the issue. Ask yourself pointed questions: *Are you upset/anxious because your boyfriend/girlfriend/spouse hasn't replied?* Then unpack your feelings. If you can recognize catastrophic thinking, try to walk yourself down by asking questions such as: *Is this true? Am I 100 percent sure this is true? What actual proof do I have?* Call the person or talk face-to-face to verify. If this isn't possible now, talk to a friend and express your feelings and concerns, but let your friend know that you're not looking for someone to validate your catastrophic stories or worst-case scenarios. Then make a list of other reasons why someone is not getting back to you—i.e., they are busy at work or with their family, they simply forgot, or they need time to themselves.

- **Set boundaries and enforce them.** If your teenager is navigating a romantic relationship via text, then boundaries are imperative. Teenagers will be more likely to follow the rules if they are consistently enforced. It can't be something done on the fly. Many families utilize "Technology Contracts" that children and parents sign, agreeing to various rules of engagement. *Psychology Today* offers one on their website: "The Best Technology-Screen Time Contract for Kids" includes language for establishing screen-time rules for school nights and weekends, with language such as: "Our family shuts down all our devices at _____ o'clock. The devices remain off until the next morning. Devices will not be turned back on until everyone has finished breakfast and is dressed and ready to leave." It also has parameters for weekends and holidays, vacations, black-out times (with options for meals together, family gatherings, friends visiting, playdates, sleepovers, walking, or driving). It also offers a variety of "alternatives" to screen time, such as choosing from three weekly activities that don't include screens—such as exercise, sports, musical instruments, art, dance, reading. It even contains acceptable search criteria for the web and social media behavior. It ends with an agreed-upon consequence for when the contract is broken and asks that both the child and parents sign, date, and agree.[7]

- **Practice what you preach**. Teens are more likely to follow your lead. If you want to make sure your kids learn how to engage more with face-to-face conversation in their relationship, then you must be willing to lead by example. That means putting the phone away when you're with your spouse/partner and not sleeping with the phone either.

- **Don't argue over text or try to resolve conflict through texting.** Why introduce so much risk for misunderstanding when things are already tough? Not surprisingly, a 2013 study by researchers at Brigham Young University found that couples who do try to hash out big issues over text report lower relationship satisfaction.[8]

- **Use texts to send loving messages.** That same study found that when partners sent each other sweet messages via text they had higher relationship satisfaction. While that may not be surprising, what was unexpected was that *sending* a nice text was associated with an even higher level of relationship satisfaction than receiving one was. Let that inspire you to use your texts to your main squeeze to express love and not just to work out logistics or share updates.

DCS in Long-term Relationships

It's not just teens and young adults who struggle with Dyscommunication in romantic relationships. Even in marriages, learning to decipher your partner's electronic communication style presents a whole new area rife with the potential to misunderstand or offend the other. Writing in shorthand and emojis can take out not just the romance but also the intentions behind everyday interactions, creating ample opportunities for disconnection to take root.

Another factor that electronic communications—particularly texting—introduces into long-term relationships is that partners often have different expectations for, and styles of, communicating electronically (just like they can have different expectations for, and styles of, just about anything in life—money, parenting, work, leisure). This can add another layer of things to be negotiated; when one partner expects the other to be reachable at all times, and the other partner keeps their phone at the bottom of their bag and forgets to check it more than once or twice all day, for example. This means of communication can then become a potential for disconnection.

Your electronic communications to each other introduce more ambiguity into your conversations and more opportunities for your different styles to manifest; electronic communications from other people are also likely interfering in your couple time. In a 2014 study of 143 married or cohabitating women, researchers found that 62 percent said technology interferes with their leisure time together.[9] In addition:

- 40 percent said their partner gets distracted by the TV during a conversation.
- 35 percent said their partner will pull out their phone if they receive a notification, even if the couple is in the middle of a conversation.

- 33 percent said their partner checks their phone during mealtimes they spend together.
- 25 percent said their partner actively texts other people during the couple's face-to-face conversations.

Of course, it's a good idea to create rules around the ways you interact with technology both together and separately. This can be done with the same or similar guidelines used for agreements between parents and children.

Self-Assessment Tool #5: How Much Are My Romantic Relationships Being Affected by Dyscommunication?

Do you or a loved one:

1) Feel preoccupied with text messages? Either thinking about previous text messages or anticipating the next one?
2) Feel the need to text constantly?
3) Feel restless, moody, depressed, anxious, or irritable when waiting for a reply?
4) Catastrophize and create elaborate narratives about why someone is not getting back to you?
5) Feel the need to respond immediately? Or feel that OTHERS need to be constantly available to respond?
6) Constantly check the phone even when it does not ring or vibrate?

7) Feel as though you have risked the loss of a significant relationship because of your behavior on the phone?

8) Feel anxious, ashamed, guilty, or depressed as a result of texts you have sent or thoughts you have had about texts?

9) Experience physical symptoms—stomach upset, heart palpitations, loss of sleep, sweating, headaches, backaches, or a sense of feeling out of control as a result of unreturned or ambiguous messages?

10) Act out in a way that causes deep shame or regret or has affected others, especially your romantic partner?

CHAPTER 6

Family

The first text came in at 4 a.m. All six sisters were on the thread.

"Mom just called. Dad is having a heart attack! I told her to hang up and call 911," Marg, the second youngest of the six sisters typed out quickly to Patty, Maura, Sage, Elle, and Suzy. The text thread was the fastest way to relay the info to everyone.

Patty, the oldest, who was up early getting ready for her morning shift as a nurse, was brushing her teeth when she saw the blue light indicating a new text pop up on her home screen. Though she and her sisters texted constantly throughout the day and evening, it wasn't like her sisters to be up this early texting. *Something is wrong!* she thought immediately as she scrambled around looking for her contacts.

Just then another text popped in. This one was from Suzy, the youngest. "What are you talking about? I am here in Mom and Dad's house!"

And then another came in.

"Go upstairs!!!! Check on Mom and Dad!" Marg texted rapidly. "Mom is calling 911. I'm on my way over with Elle. Be there in three minutes. GO UPSTAIRS!"

Suzy, who had just graduated from college, was now living in her parents' basement, two floors below their bedroom.

"Why the heck didn't she just yell for me? Why did Mom call Marg?" Suzy huffed as she ran up the two flights of stairs. She was already impossibly irritated that her mother had thought to call her sister and not her. She was sick of being iced out by her mom for her older sister Marg, who she called "Daddy's Favorite." She knew she was the family screwup—having so many school loans, working two jobs, and living at home. But surely, she thought, being *inside* the same house put her in the position to be the one called when there was a crisis?

By the time Suzy arrived upstairs and found her mother bent over her father doing chest compressions, she was irate with the entire situation.

"MOVE, MOM!" Suzy yelled. "Call 911!"

"I did! They told me to do this!" Maggie, their mom, cried out as she stood up and Suzy took over.

Suzy's phone was in her back pocket and she could feel it buzzing while she pressed repeatedly on her dad's chest, all the while yelling, "Dad! Dad! Stay with us! Dad! It's me, Suzy!"

Marg was already in the car on her way over. She and Elle, sisters number four and five, lived together in an apartment that was just minutes from their parents' home. Marg and Elle were inseparable. They worked out together, went on double dates with guys together, and knew everything about each other. While Marg drove, Elle texted the rest of the sisters—Patty, the oldest, Maura, the second oldest, and Sage, the third in the birth order.

"Suzy's there. We *finally* got her to wake up," Elle typed to the group, while Marg sped through the small Connecticut town center. "And we are on our way to the house. We hear the ambulance headed their way," Elle typed again.

In the meantime, Patty got her contacts in, saw the messages, and was finally able to respond. "I'll meet you at the hospital. On my way in to work right now. Will be there STAT. Everyone stay CALM. Everything is going to be all right!" This was classic "Positive Patty." As the oldest sister, she often looked after all of her younger siblings as if she was their mother—drying their eyes over scraped knees when they were kids and then again when they were going through heartbreaks when they were teenagers. Now that she was in her early thirties and a mom herself, she still felt responsible for keeping all her younger sisters relaxed and happy. It was also the nurse in her. She was trained to be the calm amidst the storm.

"Are you kidding me with this now, Patty?" Maura chimed in. "Stay CALM? Really? Really? Dad is having a heart attack!!!"

Maura, the second oldest and wife of a police officer, was in no mood to be told to stay calm by her older sister over text. If ever there was a time to freak out, Maura thought, this was the time. She had long been established the "worrier" of all the sisters. As a child, she kept them all awake on numerous occasions, worrying about all the things that could go wrong in the world. Since their dad was a firefighter, every time she heard sirens go out from the town center, she would be in hysterics and couldn't be soothed until their father called and let everyone know he was indeed fine.

"All I am saying is we don't know anything yet! Just stay CALM. Getting worked up never helped anyone!" Patty texted quickly to Maura and the rest of the text thread.

Maura was infuriated with Patty's missive. *She clearly didn't understand the severity of this situation,* Maura thought. But she didn't bother responding to Patty. She would handle her later. Instead she wrote, "What's going on? Suzy? What's happening? Elle? Marg? Are you there yet? What the hell is happening?" Maura couldn't bear being kept out of the loop. Her mind was reeling and as it spun out, she sent text after text, blowing up everyone's phone.

As soon as Marg and Elle got to their parents' house, they ran up the stairs to the bedroom.

"Move!" Marg yelled at Suzy and took over. Marg was already crying and upset. The entire way over to the house, she had expected the worst—she imagined her strong father lying lifeless on the ground. And it was exactly as she pictured it. Though everyone joked that Marg was Dad's favorite, Marg believed everyone was just jealous because the two were good friends and spent so much time together. Since she had dropped out of college and decided to take a job at a local restaurant, she spent her days helping him in his garden and with all the projects around the house that he had taken on since his retirement from the fire department. The thought of losing her dad and friend in this moment was beyond horrifying to her. She was also angry at Suzy for not waking up when their mother called out for her.

"Get out of here, Suzy!" Marg yelled. "God! We can't count on you for *anything*!"

Suzy, devastated, grabbed her phone out of her back pocket and ran downstairs to meet the ambulance. In an attempt to feel helpful, she decided to text everyone and update them in real time.

"Marg took over doing compressions. We'll all meet at the hospital," she typed. Then adding apropos of nothing, "It's not my fault! It's not! I can't hear anything in the basement!"

"What do you mean? We know it's not your fault," Patty said, unaware of what Marg had accused Suzy of, off the thread, just moments earlier.

Meanwhile, Elle helped her mother down the stairs and put her in the car to take her and Suzy to the hospital. "Marg can ride in the ambulance with Dad. We'll meet Patty. She's supposed to be on duty at the hospital."

When they all got in the car, after looking around at all the passengers as if doing a head count, Elle said to everyone, "Hey? Has anyone heard from Sage? Where the hell is Sage?"

Sage was the middle sister. Sage, the freewheeling and free-spirited third oldest, wasn't always the easiest to get ahold of. She was not-so-lovingly referred to as the Family Hippy. She didn't text much, but when she did, it was to laugh off her older sister Maura's daily worries and warnings. She was the first one to reply to anyone's complaints or worries with emojis and memes with affirmations like "Good Vibes Only" or "Be Here Now!" Though she meant only to calm everyone down like Patty, it only served to infuriate Maura the Worrier even more. And invariably it caused Maura to go behind Sage's back to complain to Patty or her younger sisters about how insensitive and clueless Sage was. "She thinks she's so much better than us with all of her meditation crap! I see right through her act! She's just being a bitch!"

This time though, Maura took her annoyance at her younger sister's refusal to reply directly to the text thread. "HELLO! SAGE! YOUR FATHER IS DYING! HELLO! Sorry to inconvenience you! Namaste," she wrote, not even trying to disguise her anger.

Then nothing. Sage still didn't reply.

"Just call her!" Maggie shouted out. "Goodness, girls, now is not the time to bicker. Your father is sick! You're all best friends. You're supposed to support each other, not tear each other down. Now stop it!"

Elle grabbed her phone and tried calling Sage. "No answer. Bet her phone is off."

They were at least right about that. Sage's phone was in fact off. But what they didn't know was Sage was out of town at a weekend-long retreat with a couple of her girlfriends from her yoga studio. She usually told her sisters where she was going and what she was up to, but this time it was such a last-minute decision and for such a short period of time she didn't think it would be necessary to say anything. Besides, she knew how much it pissed Maura off to talk about meditation and yoga. She didn't want to cause any problems or upset anyone on a text thread.

Meanwhile Elle, Suzy, and Maggie arrived and met Patty, who was already at the hospital in her scrubs, ready for action. Maura, who came from her own home, pulled in right behind the rest of them. Four of the six sisters were there together when they saw their dad on a gurney being rushed through the doors with Marg beside him, holding his hand. After the doctors took over and wheeled their dad into the O.R., the five sisters all hugged their mom and consoled each other. But it was clear to all of them someone was missing—Sage.

Over the course of the next hour, frantic calls and texts went out. On top of now worrying about their dad, they were all suddenly genuinely concerned about Sage. Everyone knew she was an early riser. She most certainly was up by now and had read all their texts. Not hearing from her set off several alarm bells.

Maura was at once worried and infuriated. "This is so typical of her! Here we should be worried about Dad, but now we're all worried she's dead in a ditch somewhere," she texted Patty, who was sitting just opposite of her in the waiting room, because she didn't want to say out loud what she was thinking in front of their mother.

Patty replied, "Don't worry, Maura. I am sure she's all right."

Maura replied, "Don't tell me what to do! Just because you're the oldest, you don't know everything!"

Upset now with both Sage and Patty, Maura moved on and texted Elle and Marg: "I can't even believe Sage right now. You know she's probably with some lowlife having sex and oblivious to all of this! And you know she'll come waltzing in here and make it all about herself! I can't stand it!"

"Oh, we won't let that happen! IF and WHEN she texts, we won't let her up here. Screw her. She never cared about Dad. She's the reason he had this heart attack. All the worry he's had to do over her over the years. It's no wonder he's so sick!" Marg wrote back angrily.

"Right!??? She's the reason he's in surgery right now getting cut open and god knows what else. She's so damn selfish!" Elle chimed in.

Meanwhile, Suzy, the youngest, was sitting across from the girls in the waiting room and noticed everyone texting each other. She kept looking at the sister text thread and noticed there were *no updates. Obviously*, she thought, *everyone is talking about* me *in a side text. I should have heard Mom's cries earlier. I should have done something sooner!* She felt so guilty and ashamed. And now she was certain everyone was talking about *her*. She texted Marg and Elle, "Hey, I am sorry. I didn't hear Mom this morning. I swear."

"What?" Elle wrote back. "No one blames you, Suzy!"

"Well aren't you talking about me behind my back right now? I see you all texting. But nothing is showing up on our group text thread? You're texting about me, right?"

Elle quickly typed back to Suzy, "No!!! We're not pissed at YOU! We're pissed at Sage. She's not here. She's never here. She's so damn selfish. She's the reason Dad is sick. He worries about her night and day."

Relieved the texting wasn't about her, Suzy texted back and relished having a new target in which to channel her frustration and joined in with the other sisters, "Oh, for sure! Totally agree!"

The four of them now continued to text about Sage, and all agreed that when and if Sage were to show up at the hospital, they wouldn't let her come in to see their dad.

Patty was unaware of any of these side texts from her younger sisters about Sage. Instead, she was more concerned about how her father was doing and kept checking in with her colleagues at the nurses' station.

She was standing beside some nurses when she got a text from Sage.

"Ohmygosh! I just turned my phone on! I am at a silent retreat! How's Dad?" Sage texted furiously as she pulled out of the retreat center in her car.

"First of all. He's alive." Patty delivered the good news first. She had been on the other end of lots of these types of texts and knew what to say first.

"Oh, thank god," Sage took her eyes off the road and typed, looked up briefly, and then read the incoming text from Patty.

"But you need to get here soon! He's in surgery now. We don't know what's going on. We haven't heard anything in a while. He was in bad shape when they brought him in. Can you get here ASAP?"

Sage read quickly and saw "really bad shape" and panicked. While pushing the accelerator she typed, "I am two hours from home. I am already in the car driving. I will floor it and get there as fast as I …" Sage heard a loud horn blast and looked up from her phone and slammed on her brakes just in time. Without realizing it, she had blown through a red light at an intersection and barely missed a jogger crossing the street. If it hadn't been for that stranger's horn, she most definitely would have struck and killed the man at the speed she was going. Shaking from the shock of it, Sage pulled over to the side of the road. The news of her father's heart attack, trying to stay in communication via text, and now almost killing someone because she was texting and driving was just too much for her to handle. She knew she needed to take a minute and collect herself before getting back on the road. She also knew she had to turn off her phone. If she were going to make it to the hospital safely, she couldn't be texting and driving.

Just after Patty finished texting Sage, a doctor from the O.R. approached her and let her know her father's condition. He told Patty her father suffered serious damage to his heart, he was in critical condition, and he might not survive the surgery. He assured her that he and his team were going to try to do everything they could to save her father, but the prognosis wasn't great. As a nurse, Patty recognized the look in the doctor's eyes. There would be no sugarcoating this message. Even she, Positive Patty, couldn't make this sound good. She didn't want to put something so serious in a text. She just had to tell her sisters and mother the truth in person and prepare them should the worst happen. She rushed down the hall and delivered the news to her family, all the while forgetting that she had just texted with Sage. She was so preoccupied with delivering the bad news, she forgot to mention that Sage was on her way to the hospital.

So, Maura, Elle, Marg, and Suzy, now fearing the worst for their father, continued to text back and forth all morning about Sage's thoughtlessness in not being there with the rest of them.

Two hours later a text finally came in from Sage to the entire group.

"Hey guys. Where are you? The ER? Or some other waiting area? Let me know so I can find you!"

Maura seized on the text.

"Don't bother," Maura texted back quickly.

"What?" Sage texted back, confused, unaware of the faction that had been forming behind her and Patty's backs while she was driving.

"We don't want you here! You have no business showing up here NOW," Maura texted back. "Took you long enough!"

Sage was crushed. *What were they talking about?* She loved her sisters. She loved her father. *What is happening? Did I do something wrong?* She had explained to Patty why her phone was off. She was at a retreat. And then she did the best she could to get there as fast as she could. But after almost hitting the jogger, Sage had decided to turn her phone off and drive more carefully. After all, the family didn't need another crisis to deal with.

Patty, who was sitting across from Maura, shouted across the room. "Maura! What are you doing? Why would you say that to Sage? She's as welcome here as any one of us!"

"You know damn well she doesn't care about Dad! She shows up when it's good for her!" Maura shouted back.

Marg, Elle, and Suzy nodded in agreement. They had all been discussing the various reasons why Sage wasn't welcome all morning over texts and had done a terrific job of convincing themselves that Sage wasn't just a terrible sister, daughter, and friend, but she was a terrible person who was actually not responding to their texts as a way to get more attention and sympathy, not to mention cause further worry and panic. *She's such a drama queen! Always plays the victim! Just you wait and see! She'll make it all about her.*

"This is crazy!" Patty said. She picked up her phone and began to text Sage. "We're on the ..." when Maura lunged across the room and grabbed the phone from Patty. "How dare you? We told you, Patty, we don't want Sage here!"

Patty was confused because she hadn't been on all the side-texts and was unaware of where all this rage from her younger sisters was coming from.

"She's our sister! What's wrong with you people!" Patty shouted.

Meanwhile, Sage was sitting in her car in the parking lot, staring at her phone and watching as three dots blinked. It was clear Patty was in the middle of typing something to her. This calmed Sage for a moment. *Clearly, there was some mistake. The first texts from Maura weren't meant for me.* Sage was waiting for Patty to clarify the misunderstanding and find out where they were in the hospital.

Back on the third-floor waiting room, a surgeon walked in and interrupted the sisters' fight over text messages that should or shouldn't be sent. He closed the door of the waiting room behind him and sat down next to the women. This got all their attention.

"He's not out of the woods, but he made it. We just need to wait and see. We've moved him to the ICU, where we'll be monitoring him closely," the doctor said seriously.

The girls burst out in tears of both relief and dread. *He's not dead! But, ICU?!*

"If you'd all like to come in and see him, we can do that now. Only one of you can enter his room at a time," the doctor said as he stood up.

The sisters and their mother collected themselves, hugged each other, and followed the surgeon down the long corridors.

They gathered as they looked through the window of the ICU room, where their father was recuperating. Suddenly, all their petty squabbles over texts dissipated.

Meanwhile, Sage sat in her car waiting for a reply from Patty. Finally, when she couldn't wait another second, she texted back.

"Where are you guys? Hello?"

Unbeknownst to Sage, they were all with their father. She thought of calling them but was so worried and anxious about Maura's text. Sage was scared to talk to any of them now. They seemed upset with her. *I know I'm late, but they couldn't be that mad about that, could they?* It just made no sense. Too nervous now to reply, she thought she would go look for them in the hospital on her own.

When she finally got to the ICU, she saw her sisters walking down the hall.

She could tell in all their faces they were annoyed with her. When she approached them all, Maura, Marg, Elle, and Suzy iced her out and didn't even look at her. Patty was the only one to embrace her. Alone, confused, and in pain from the grief, Sage asked why everyone was mad at her.

Maura shouted, "Are you really going to make this all about you right now? What did I tell you girls? Dad is in ICU, and Sage wants to know why we're mad at her! It's always all about *her*!"

Sage was devastated. She didn't understand how or why the girls were angry.

Patty jumped in between Sage and Maura and the rest of the sisters and explained that Sage was at a retreat, that she had texted her—Patty—and she had forgotten to tell the rest of the group amidst all the commotion.

"I honestly tried to get here as fast as I could! I almost killed someone I was going so fast and trying to text you all," Sage explained.

"Oh," Maura said flatly, feeling embarrassed and ashamed for her behavior all morning.

"We had no idea," Marg chimed in.

"It's okay, it was all a big misunderstanding," Patty said. "We're all here now. And Dad needs us to be here with Mom and each other. Right now. In this moment. Let's just put the phones away. Enough already! We're all together and alive and that's what matters."

Dyscommunication Is More than Unreturned Messages

This story of a family in distress clearly illustrates what I mean when I use the term Dyscommunication crisis. A family is torn apart on a father's deathbed and a near-accident that could have killed somebody occurs because of Dyscommunication.

Dyscommunication is more than an unreturned message or a delayed message. If you were to tell someone that a "delay" in communication could cause a full-blown crisis, they might laugh at you or appear puzzled. The real problem here, as we all now understand the neocortex's role, is that we've lost an immediate feedback loop. We have been so used to communicating with immediate feedback. We could just jump on a phone. There was an immediate closure to the loop. If a response was unclear or ambiguous, we could clarify it on the spot. As we now know, our brain is wired to seek a closed connection. And when the closure is not there, we feel lost without it. With texts and emails there is *always a delay*. The messages are incomplete. This is what has created the Dyscommunication crisis. But just returning a message does not mean the communication loop is closed. Especially with texts, the returned text can still leave us unclear, forcing our minds to spin just like they would with an unreturned message.

Most of our communication today is through email and text. Misunderstanding takes place on these platforms rather than in person or over the phone. And that's why there are so many misunderstandings. It's *Dyscommunication*. Texts and emails breed misunderstandings because we can't rely on the immediate feedback loop of the past. Most misunderstandings today are Dyscommunication, due to the intrinsic problems of digital communication.

What happened between this group of sisters happens more often than most are aware. Many families have group text threads now. Many relationships, familial or otherwise, now completely exist digitally. And texting and communicating digitally is chock full of opportunities for Dyscommunication. "Misunderstandings" are "Dyscommunication" if the medium is digital. Simple communications that once could be handled over the phone or in person have now been relegated to texts or emails. Simply scheduling a lunch can take a week now if done so digitally. And doing so brings with it all kinds of attitudes, drama, and resentments, i.e., who is compromising and who is not, who is more invested in the relationship and who is not, who responds and who doesn't, etc.

In group texts, it's also so easy for factions to develop: all one has to do is jump off a group text thread and start a side text thread. And this happens even over innocuous events such as planning lunches, events, and parties! Just imagine what navigating deep interpersonal relationships over text can be like. It can be rife with proverbial landmines. Old resentments, paranoia, delusional scenarios, thinking the worst of our friends and family members, and assuming all sorts of terrible motives and behaviors are more common than not. Ask any teenager or millennial to list the number of fights they've had over text, and you'd be hard pressed to find someone who doesn't have to use more than one hand to count all the times texting quickly escalated or got out of hand. Many people can even count the number of friendships they've lost because of texting that got out of control. Others can attest to ostracizing someone simply due to text messages. There are so many ways for our minds to go haywire when communicating digitally. If it's not misreading the tone or meaning of a text, it could be a lack of context that keeps a message from being read clearly; either way, misunderstandings are bound to happen over texts. Add to this what we already know of how our brain works when confronted with broken loops in our already complex relationships, and communicating digitally is like adding an accelerant to a fire.

Of course, so many of these fights could easily be solved by picking up the phone and talking in person immediately, instead of jumping to conclusions. But, alas, that's easier said than done. As in the case of these sisters, Marg thought it would be best if she just texted everyone, so she didn't have to call them individually. She was pressed for time, and a text message to the group seemed like a great idea. It was, after all, the primary way they all had grown accustomed to communicating.

Like the sisters, we're all hungry for interpersonal connection, and it seems like we're getting it when we text; however, when we don't get answers to our texts, or the texts are ambiguous, or loaded, we in turn feel lonely or left out, which in turn inspires us to send out more and more texts, direct messages, and emails in a search of connection that only real-time, preferably face-to-face interaction, can provide. And when those communications aren't completed satisfactorily, it can make us feel even more isolated, and our thoughts can spiral about what's wrong with us.

The situation these sisters were in already was ripe for Dyscommunication. They were dealing with a completely unexpected event—their beloved father was having a heart attack and could possibly die. Talk about broken loops! Add to this mix lifelong established roles (i.e., the oldest, the youngest, the middle child), personality and identity issues (i.e., the favorite, the positive one, the worrier, the hippy), and relationship dynamics (i.e., Maura and Sage didn't get along and often butted heads, Patty felt the need to bring everyone together, and Suzy believed everyone thought she was the screwup), and it's a recipe for disaster! For example, Suzy, the screwup (identity), already felt guilty for not hearing her mother's cries, and she immediately believed everyone was texting about her behind her back. And Maura, a known worrier, was annoyed by Patty dismissing her concerns.

Everyone in this family was already filled with anxiety and agitation. They had no idea what was going to happen to their father. They also had no idea who was doing what or when. Coordinating everyone via text was probably the worst possible way to get everyone on the same page, but since texting was the mode of communication they were all so familiar with, it was their go-to communication mode in a moment of crisis. When one didn't reply (Sage), it created yet another broken loop. A faction quickly developed. Maura, the self-professed worrier of the group, who already had lifelong issues with Sage, created this faction by including her other sisters to revolt against Sage. Having a scapegoat and someone to direct her ire at felt good. It certainly felt better than focusing on the unknown status of her ailing father. It didn't take long for the faction to slip into a full-blown DCS—taking Sage's lack of response personally, resenting her, and distrusting her, and then catastrophizing and accusing her of sleeping with a "lowlife" and choosing not to respond in order to make it all about her. Eventually, they did something they all came to regret—they iced their sister out completely and told her she wasn't welcome to see their dad.

It wasn't until they all saw each other face-to-face that Patty was able to clear up in real time the reason Sage was out of the loop for so long that morning. And Sage could also explain the situation herself. After all, she nearly killed someone trying to keep up with the texts while driving!

Dyscommunication Kills

In the story, there is a near-fatal traffic accident due to texting and driving. In 2018, 4,637 deaths were caused by distracted driving in the U.S., which accounts for over 9 percent of all fatal crashes.[1] Texting and driving is six times more likely to lead to car accidents than driving under the influence.[2] In other words, texting and driving is more dangerous than drinking and driving! Just how dangerous? Sending one text message takes about five to seven seconds, which is more than enough time to travel a hundred yards—the length of a football field.[3] And it's not just fatalities that should concern us: according to the CDC, 416,000 individuals in 2019 were injured in accidents involving a distracted driver.[4] You would think there would be laws against this, since they are so dangerous. And you would be right. Texting and driving is prohibited in forty-seven states and the fines can be extremely high. Yet still people feel the compulsion to text back immediately—even when it threatens their own life and the lives of others. In fact, a recent report by Edgar Snyder estimates there are roughly 660,000 drivers right now using smartphones while driving. That means currently in the U.S. there are well over a half a million distracted drivers on the road.[5] Interestingly enough, one of the most common reasons why drivers text and drive is to respond to work-related messages.[6] Though it seemed like Sage was only texting and driving in the above story because of an "emergency," the reality is most people aren't texting and driving because they're dealing with real emergencies, rather they're carrying on rather banal conversations and work-related matters—all of which can wait. Regardless, whether one feels the need to respond to a text because it's an emergency or not, it's dangerous and can cause a serious crisis—or even death.

Though it's clear from this story there was a lot going on in real life that contributed to the anxiety and agitation of all people involved, the syndrome was exacerbated by texting and communicating digitally. However, things don't have to get this out of hand. Here are some ways to mitigate Dyscommunication in families:

1) **Whenever possible, take it offline.** In other words: spend some time on the phone or in person. If the entire relationship is digital, you may want to consider how you communicate and maintain your relationship. So much of the Dyscommunication between these sisters didn't have to happen at all. Their entire text thread was filled with misunderstandings, ambiguous responses, and uncompleted loops. As a result, there was side texting, accusations, catastrophizing, and all sorts of regrettable and shameful behavior. Talking in person is the best way to make plans and arrangements, and it's the best way to talk about feelings, especially in the heat of the moment.

2) **Check in and do so with empathy, rather than accusations.** No one asked Sage if she was okay. They jumped immediately to accusations. Simply asking someone if everything is okay can show that person that you care about them and that your reason for texting them isn't hostile. Even acknowledging that a person may be busy

is helpful. Ask them: *Is this a good time to text? Or do you have the energy to text right now?* This acknowledges that you respect your friend's time and space. She was away and didn't know they were looking for her. Then she was in her car and unavailable to respond.

3) **Take a minute and realize that a person may not be texting because they are busy doing something else, like driving.** Texting can feel intrusive and sometimes like an ambush, especially group texts, in which dozens of texts can flood in during a short period of time. Since texting is a mode of conversation that mimics real conversation, people have the expectation that others should be immediately available to respond. The reality is most of us *can't* respond to texts or emails immediately. We all have work, lives, and a myriad of responsibilities. Sometimes, we are even driving a car! As I said earlier, it's against the law in most states to text and drive, yet most people admit to doing so. The Department of Transportation reported in 2019 that 4,637 people died while texting and driving.[7] Though 97 percent of drivers agree and acknowledge that texting and emailing while driving is dangerous, 43 percent still do it. [8] The compulsion to respond immediately and close our broken loops is so strong, we often are willing to risk our own lives and the lives of others to do so. Giving people the space to respond on their own time helps alleviate the pressure on both sides to respond right away. Whatever it is, it can wait. Even an emergency. It's not worth your life or the lives of others to text and drive. If Sage hadn't

stopped her car in time, she could have killed someone, and the family would suddenly have two crises on their hands. If you have trouble self-regulating, let technology help. Today there are several apps and phone services that automatically respond for you while you're driving. They send out pre-written messages when an incoming text message or email arrives, and the message explains you're driving and can't respond at this time. There are also text blocker apps, which disable the ability to text when a vehicle is going over ten mph.

4) **Setting clear boundaries and rules of engagement is imperative.** This is especially important with group texts and emails. Side texting and talking behind people's backs never ends well. Invariably the person who is being talked about will find out, especially since we can all screenshot and save messages. As they say, "We keep the receipts!" In other words, it's quite easy for someone to screen capture negative or hurtful things and share them—causing even more hurt. The adage holds true: *If you can't say it front of them, don't say it behind them.* If you have an issue with someone, it's best to pick up the phone and ask them first if they're okay—and once that is established, then ask them why they aren't responding or if something is amiss. If you've established a routine where you text every day with someone, and then that suddenly doesn't happen, you can bet it will cause tension or worry. It's best to be proactive and let people know if you're going to be out of pocket or there is going to be a change in the routine. Letting people

know ahead of time mitigates a lot of anxiety. If Sage had just let her sisters know she was out of town, they wouldn't have jumped to so many false conclusions and could have waited for her arrival. Automating outboxes also helps alleviate anxiety.

5) **Create more productive digital conversations by responding to a friend's email or text directly.** Sometimes, texts can come in fast and it's hard to keep up. Be sure to read through an entire message before responding and then follow up on items. If it's an email, you can respond in the body of their email in a different color or in italics with comments such as "This reminds me of the time we got lost on the way home from the mall!" or "I had totally forgotten about that!" This way the exchange is more interactive. In texts, it's okay to say: *"Hold up! I can't keep up with the stream!* Or *"What did you say?"* Or follow up specifically: *"Did you just say Dad had a heart attack? What happened? Can we talk on the phone now instead of text?"* Following up with specifics shows a person you're reading everything and you're engaged. It also lessens chances for misreading things or not readings things altogether. If it's extremely serious or timely, picking up the phone to talk is even more vital.

Self-Assessment Tool #6: How Much Is My Family Being Affected by Dyscommunication?

Do you:

1) Feel anxious about the amount of text messages and feel like you can't keep up?
2) Side text or use text messages to talk about others behind their backs and escalate situations?
3) Feel anxious or irritable when waiting for a reply?
4) Feel compelled to immediately respond? Have you found yourself texting with your friends while driving because it feels like an urgent reply is required?
5) Catastrophize and create elaborate narratives about why someone is not getting back to you?
6) Feel that your family relationships are suffering because you're spending too much time texting and not enough time in person?
7) Feel like something is missing in your family because the nature of your relationships is completely digital?
8) Say things you regret or make terrible assumptions that you would never say in person but feel free to do so through texts?
9) Gang up or create a faction using text to ice someone out?
10) Act out in a way that causes deep shame or regret or causes the loss of a relationship with a family member?

CHAPTER 7

Work

"Whatever you do, don't talk to Ben this morning. He's on a warpath. Avoid at all costs! Remember, you didn't hear it from me." Kyle read the email from his coworker Scott, who was sitting right across from him. Though they sat in proximity, they rarely talked. Instead they emailed each other throughout the day so their boss, Ben, and other colleagues couldn't hear their ongoing conversations.

Kyle didn't need Scott's email to read the room. From the moment he walked into the large, spacious, open-concept office that morning, Kyle could feel the tension as if they were stuffed into a small cubicle. He also could see that Ben, who was high up in the loft above, was typing furiously. In fact, everyone in the office could hear the aggressive clacking of Ben's keyboard.

"Let's hope he's not sending that email to us," Kyle typed back to Scott.

"No kidding. Hey, have you heard from Joe yet? Wonder if he is coming in today. I heard he was 'sick' yesterday," Scott typed, quickly putting the word *sick* in quotes to emphasize his doubts about his coworker's illness.

"No idea. Wouldn't surprise me if he called in again today. Typical. We're on a deadline and you know Joe: First to leave, last to arrive. Must be nice not to give a shit," Kyle emailed back quickly.

Scott and Kyle had been working at the firm together for ten years and had fully embraced their boss's culture of "he who stays the latest cares the most and deserves to be the next partner." Their coworker Joe, who had been in the firm the longest, wasn't as driven as Kyle and Scott though. Joe had the punch-in-punch-out mentality and was always racing to get home to his wife and kids. He also didn't feel the need to work as hard as the younger guys on the team. As an old friend of Ben's, Joe was confident he would be made partner just by virtue of his seniority.

"Wonder if that is why Ben is so pissed," Scott wrote and then looked up again at the loft where Ben was indignantly typing.

It was easy for everyone in the office to see Ben was agitated. There were no barriers or walls at all between desks—and even the loft's railing that surrounded Ben's desk was glass. This way Ben, the principal architect and designer of the firm of nearly thirty architects, could look out from his seat and keep his eye on everyone below without ever having to stand up. While most offices are designed with open concepts to help foster collaboration, this wasn't the reason why Ben had designed it this way. In fact, he hated to hear small talk or banter of any kind. Instead he encouraged absolute silence and required monk-like focus and dedication from his employees throughout the day. As a result, most of his employees moved their conversations on-line—primarily through emails and texts. It was a win-win for them. They all knew it appeared to Ben that they were working throughout the day, and of course they all enjoyed never having to get up and talk to anyone in person.

Unbeknownst to Kyle and Scott, Ben had just received a dis-turbing email from his longest-serving employee and friend, Joe.

"I am not coming in again."

Ben was furious. Immediately, he understood the email to mean that Joe was quitting and leaving the firm high and dry in the middle of a huge project and deadline. Ben didn't think he misread the email and believed that "I'm not coming in again" meant Joe wasn't just out sick for another day, but rather, he was in fact never coming back to the office. Ben was furious. *To think, after all I have done for him, he wouldn't even give me two weeks' notice!? Of all the insubordinate, lazy, ungrateful, and unprofessional things to do. And to think I was going to name him partner!* Ben seethed.

Ben then sent an email to the office manager, Craig, who sat downstairs below with the others. "Joe just quit. No notice. Nothing. Says he's not coming in again. Stop all payments. Health insurance. All of it. Shut down his workstation. Divide all his assignments between Kyle and Scott in the interim. Cancel bonus payout and vacation pay. Call lawyers and cease partner contract negotiations."

"What?" Craig typed back quickly. "Did he say why?"

"No. Nothing. He's left us high and dry," Ben typed back. "We're screwed. We have a deadline on Friday. So typical of Joe."

"Did you call him? Make sure he's okay? That something isn't seriously wrong with him? I know he's a bit relaxed, but he has a wife and two kids. He can't just quit," Craig asked incredulously.

Then, while waiting for a reply from Ben, Craig quickly emailed his friend Scott. "Ben says Joe just quit."

Scott perked up in his chair and quickly forwarded the email from Craig on to Kyle.

"No shit!" Kyle emailed back to Scott. "I didn't think he had it in him to quit! No wonder Ben is furious!"

Meanwhile, Scott quickly grabbed his phone and surreptitiously texted Joe. "Dude! You just up and quit! What's up? What happened! Details, man. Ben is losing it here!"

Back at his home, Joe was nearly catatonic. The flu that had already ravaged its way from his wife to his kids was now working its way through him. He could barely move. Every muscle in his body ached, and he had a fever of 103. He heard his phone buzz, but he assumed it was just some work emails and dismissed them. He had emailed Ben first thing that morning, so he knew everyone would just pick up the slack until he returned. Then he heard the phone buzz again. This time, however, Joe simply couldn't ignore it. Groggily, he rolled over and grabbed his phone and read a text from Scott.

"Quit? I didn't quit," Josh said aloud, alarmed now. He quickly opened and read the full text from Scott and started responding.

"I didn't quit. Very sick. Just not coming in today," Joe replied wearily, unable to write in complete sentences.

Scott read Joe's text and screenshot it and sent it on to Kyle for a laugh.

Kyle texted back, "I don't think Ben knows that" and then pointed up to Ben still furiously typing up at his computer.

Just then a company-wide email was sent to everyone in the firm—the subject line read: "Joe." The email went on to say: "Effective Immediately: Joe is no longer employed at G.G.&L Architects. Work orders have changed. See below."

Everyone's heads looked up from their screens to stare up at Ben.

"What are you all looking at!" Ben shouted. "Back to work! We're on deadline!"

"Sir, um, Ben," Scott began to speak, but he saw his friend Kyle shaking his head as if to say, *Do not get involved. This could be your chance.* Scott heeded the warning and said nothing. With Joe gone, now it meant he was a step closer to partner himself. *Yes, maybe this could be good for me,* he thought.

Kyle, feeling the need to stir things up, forwarded the company-wide email on to Joe, forgetting that Joe was in fact on the original email thread.

Back at home, still delirious with a fever, Joe was now opening his sent emails to see if he had mistakenly quit in the middle of the night during a fever-induced hallucination. He read and reread his email to Ben. *Wasn't I perfectly clear? I said I wasn't coming in* again. *I was sick yesterday, so the word* again *clearly refers to today. How did he get I am quitting from that message? God, he's such a freak. He's always flying off the handle. Why can't the dude just chill out?*

Just then Joe saw two emails come in—one was a company-wide email and the other was from Kyle, who had forwarded him the company-wide email with a note: "What's up with this? Why did you quit?" *What?! How in the world can this be happening?* Joe scrambled out of bed and to his feet. He grabbed his phone and quickly texted Ben to clear the air.

"There's been a huge misunderstanding! I'm just *sick*. I haven't quit. I have the flu. I emailed you this morning to say I wasn't coming in *again*—as in today, not as in forever."

Joe waited for a reply for several minutes and heard nothing.

Meanwhile, Ben was furious. He had wasted an entire morning of productive work because Joe couldn't be bothered with writing a proper out-of-office message or even picking up the phone to explain to him why he would be out sick. *Yes, I may have misread the email, but clearly it was an honest mistake. Everyone knows "not coming in again" means "not coming in again ever." Right?* Ben rationalized his response to himself. He was over Joe getting away with doing things half-assed and calling in sick just as a deadline was looming. He was going to teach Joe a lesson. He wasn't going to reply to Joe right away. *I'm going to make him sweat it out. Show him who is boss. That way he'll never be able to take me or this job for granted. My employees have no idea how good they have it!*

Joe was clearly annoyed now. Not hearing back from Ben was driving him nuts. *Of course, Ben did all of this on purpose. He always had it out for him because he wasn't such a kiss-ass like Scott.* Infuriated with Ben, Joe quickly typed a reply to what he thought was Kyle's forwarded company-wide email: "What a complete moron! So typical of Ben to go off the rails over

NOTHING. He's such a control freak, and yet he can't even properly read a stupid email? I didn't quit. Just a huge misunderstanding. I'll see you all tomorrow."

Joe pushed send quickly, failing to check who he was sending the response to. Suddenly, a rush of panic rose within him. *Did I click on the right conversation? Did I click on Kyle's forwarded email and reply just to him, or did I click on the company-wide email and reply to everyone? Oh shit. Shit. Shit. Shit.*

Joe checked the email and, sure enough, as if this day couldn't get any worse, he had indeed replied-all to the entire company. Everyone in the firm, including Ben, received Joe's scorching email.

Within seconds, Joe heard another alert from his phone.

"Joe, well this isn't a misunderstanding. Just so we're clear: You're fired. We'll send you your things. Signed, Your Moronic Control Freak Boss Ben"

Something Small Can Become Big

Ambiguous messages. Delayed responses. Side texting. Misunderstood messages. Office politics. Hierarchies. Add to this a side of reply-all to the wrong party and you have the perfect recipe for a full-blown Dyscommunication crisis.

So how did an innocuous calling-out-sick email result in an employee's firing? How is that possible, right? How can something so banal become so fraught with human emotion and drama? Digital communication, that's how.

Though this scenario of Ben's architecture firm is an extreme example, most offices now rely completely on email and texts and other forms of digital communications to communicate throughout the day. Yes, even in "open concept" buildings, where everyone can ostensibly speak to their coworkers without ever getting up, people still rely on emails and texts for the bulk of day-to-day communication.

In fact, the average worker spends 4.1 hours a day responding to work messages, according to a report commissioned by Adobe and reported on in the *Washington Post*.[1] Just responding! Each email represents a decision. And every "yes" frequently results in more work. While that's stressful enough, each email also represents a major opportunity for Dyscommunication.

While written communications are nothing new, the immediacy of email makes it seem more informal than it truly is, particularly in a work setting. It also lacks all nonverbal clues—facial expressions, gestures, and body language that scientists estimate convey at least 65 percent of our meaning during face-to-face conversations. And, it turns out, we are terrible at discerning the true messages that email senders intend to convey. Yet we *think* we are great at it, which makes it all the more upsetting when our email communication loops go unbroken. We even have difficulty extrapolating the meaning of basic words. As Joe's email so clearly demonstrated—something as simple as "I am not coming in again" can be understood by the receiver as "I am quitting."

If Joe had simply picked up the phone and spoken those words, "Hey, Ben, I'm not coming in again," followed by cough, cough, and a weak-sounding goodbye, any sane person would be able to quickly discern that Joe wasn't quitting, he was calling out sick. It's not just out-sick messages either that can be easily misinterpreted. Emails laced with sarcasm can easily be mistaken as well. In a 2005 study,[2] two psychology professors asked undergraduate college students to either email or speak a series of statements about generic topics while using a specific tone—either sarcasm or seriousness—to other students. The creators of the messages, both verbal and written, predicted that their tone would be successfully conveyed 78 percent of the time. The group whose messages were spoken pretty much nailed it—their messages were interpreted correctly 75 percent of the time. But those who received the messages in email form only understood the tone correctly 56 percent of the time. Turns out, email is pretty hit or miss when it comes to conveying tone. But the problem is that we *think* we're good at reading tone in emails—90 percent of the recipients thought they got it right.

And it's not just word choice and tone that are issues. We don't email each other in a vacuum. We each have our own personalities, agendas, and motivations, not to mention underlying beliefs about ourselves and others. In this architecture firm, there were several men vying for the same coveted position—partner. The boss, Ben, was trying to maintain a sense of control in his office and clearly enjoyed being considered superior and, quite literally, "above" everyone. Joe, a family man, took work just seriously enough. It was a means to an end. But it was, nevertheless, an important means. He needed to provide for his family. However, he just wasn't willing to put in all the hours Scott and Kyle did to prove his dedication to Ben and the company. Add all these personality and identity issues to the mix and the stage is set for Dyscommunication.

When people don't write clear messages, ambiguity leads to confusion, and confusion leads to broken loops, as do unreturned messages—which then lead to the typical stages.

1.   Anxiety and agitation

Ben became incensed when he read Joe's ambiguous email. He immediately became agitated and started to spin out.

2.   Taking it personally

When he first read the email, Ben's response was to take it all personally. He thought to himself: *To think, after all I have done for him, he wouldn't even give me two weeks' notice?*

3.   Resentment and distrust

What happened next is he started developing theories that, if said out loud, would sound delusional. *Of all the insubordinate, lazy, ungrateful, and unprofessional things to do. And to think I was going to name him partner!*

4.   Catastrophizing

As we know, because our mind so strongly craves a narrative that has an end point, we will create our own ending. In this case, Ben immediately saw the ambiguous email from Joe as him quitting.

5.   Possibly doing something you regret

Though Ben wouldn't admit it, sending off emails quickly to his company and business manager announcing Joe's removal from the office without talking to Joe in person first might be something he would regret in hindsight.

6. <u>Inability to talk yourself down</u>

Because the brain can't tolerate an incomplete pattern, Ben's thoughts tended to just keep looping. Ben was in a full-blown spiral, convinced of the worst, sending emails off like rockets, not even thinking about slowing down or considering other alternative scenarios, even when his office manager, Craig, advised him to call Joe and follow up.

7. <u>Feeling ashamed</u>

Ben then tried to rationalize his behavior because of the shame. *Yes, I may have misread the email, but clearly it was an honest mistake. Everyone knows "not coming in again" means "not coming in again ever." Right?*

But Ben wasn't the only one suffering from DCS. Joe immediately believed Ben was out to get him and did it all on purpose because he wasn't always "sucking up" to him like Scott and Kyle were.

And in this case Joe was right. Ben used a delayed reply to Joe as a weapon—he did it purposefully, knowing it would cause Joe to spiral and admitting to wanting Joe to "sweat it out" so he could show Joe "who was boss."

Another factor contributing to the Dyscommunication is all too common in workplaces—what is commonly referred to as the *reply-all-pocalypse,* or accidentally sending a reply-all message instead of replying directly to the intended recipient. Who hasn't replied-all to a group with a message only intended for one party and felt instant shame and regret? In this case, Joe, suffering from a severe case of DCS after not hearing back from Ben, sent off a scathing email that wasn't intended to be seen by

Ben. Unfortunately, Ben did see it and it led to Joe's termination. While Joe's email simply resulted in his firing, some reply-all scenarios have led to full-blown international crises. The U.S. State Department once crashed its email server, after one of its employees replied-all to a blank email sent to a global distribution list.[3] Large companies spend tens of millions of dollars every year on lost productivity due to reply-all emails, according to Ryan Fuller, the former vice president of Workplace Analytics at Microsoft.[4] Even worse, Fuller reports, the constant flow of information, demand on workers' attention, and frequent interruptions of emails and texts get in the way of actual productive work. Emails also stress people out and are endlessly distracting. Ben may have thought he was being the ultimate progressive boss—with an open concept office—but in reality, everyone was so afraid to talk that they spent the majority of their day texting and emailing instead of working and focusing on actual projects.

Of course, behind all of this, what is driving this Dyscommunication crisis is the sheer volume of emails and texts. According to the market research firm Radicati Group there are 235.6 billion emails sent every single day. And on any given business day, an email user will receive 125 emails. No wonder we spend four hours—half of our workday—just replying to or reading emails! The *Washington Post* even has a calculator than can predict, based on when you started work, when you expect to retire, and how often you check your email, just how many total hours you will have spent emailing in your lifetime (it could add up to around fifty thousand hours, if you're wondering). It's depressing, to say the least.

The volume alone means we shouldn't be surprised when someone hasn't gotten back to us. We're all in the same email-laden boat, and we're all sinking from the daily deluge. Even the most fastidious among us can easily overlook important emails or even relegate emails to a to-do pile with every intention of responding, only to realize when it's too late that we may have forgotten to respond. Some of us just read the subject lines and decide not to open an email altogether and instead delete them to free up our inbox space.

Most of us don't have bosses like Ben who are hotheaded, ill-suited for leadership, and purposefully refuse to respond to employees. However, many of us can relate to being so busy and wrapped up in our own to-do lists and stress that we misread emails or lash out at our peers and colleagues because we simply read too much into them or misread them altogether.

Though it's clear from what happened between Ben and Joe there was a lot more going on than Dyscommunication. Ben clearly had an inferiority complex of some sort and loved to lord over his employees and micromanage them. So much so that his employees had to call *him* when they were calling out sick instead of an HR or office manager. He was simply doing way too much. And there were a lot of office politics at play: vying for promotions and partnership can create rivalries and competition. Scott could have let Ben know right away that there was a misunderstanding between him and Joe, but he used the situation to his advantage to knock out the competition. And of course, at the heart of this Dyscommunication crisis were the ambiguous and unreturned messages. On any given day, we're given 125 opportunities to misread emails, delete them, forget to respond to them, or reply in a way that causes further misunderstandings and ultimately DCS. In the following chapter, I'll go in more depth about how to prevent Dyscommunication in all aspects of your life, but here are a few tips to help mitigate Dyscommunication at work:

1) **Whenever possible, take it offline.** If you're seeing a pattern, then good. (Your brain is probably grateful for it.) The reality is so much of the crises that occur because of Dyscommunication at work can be avoided by simply picking up a phone and/or talking in-person. And if that's not possible, at least make the effort to schedule a time to talk in-person. This is especially important if it's a highly charged or emotional issue.

2) **Keep messages short and to the point.** If a person is receiving an average of 125 emails a day, the likelihood that they have ample time to peruse a lengthy email is basically nil. If you have a key question you need answers to, quickly ask the question and let the person know a specific time you need the answer by. If you have multiple questions, consider breaking them up into multiple emails so that important or salient points aren't overlooked or totally forgotten in long emails.

3) **But don't make the messages too short or ambiguous.** Don't forget, the initial cause of the confusion in the story of Ben and Joe was that Joe's message was too vague and ambiguous. If you're writing a text or sending an email to a coworker or boss, be sure to be as clear and transparent as possible. Joe's email might have landed very differently if he had said, "Dear Ben, I am still

not feeling well. I'll be out sick again today. I'll check my email later today, but right now I need to rest. Joe." Check spelling, reread messages, and make sure you're not using sarcasm or a tone that can be misconstrued.

4) **If you're going to be away from the office, step away from your desk, go on an important call, or take time to concentrate, clearly articulate that in auto-response tools.** Simply setting up an auto reply that says something like: "I'm working on an important project until November 1 and, as a result, I'll be less responsive to my email. If you need an immediate response before that time, contact my associate [and include their contact information]. If you absolutely need my input, please email me again with 'urgent' in the subject line—the reminder will be helpful to me (and you won't be bugging me)." It'll buy you some time, and it will ease the other person's mind as well. Same goes if you're out sick or on vacation, using auto-response tools puts other people's minds at ease—it closes the loop. They won't take your lack of response personally, become anxious, or begin to catastrophize.

5) **Set up clear times of day when you check and respond to messages.** Responding to or feeling the need to respond to messages can interrupt your concentration and productivity. If you need to concentrate, turn off email notifications and set up designated times when you check and respond to emails, so your colleagues and coworkers can know when to expect responses. Or if you're an early riser and like to work first thing in the morning, let your colleagues know that is when

you'll be checking and responding to emails, but you by no means expect them to get back to you at 4:30 a.m. Setting clear boundaries and expectations also ameliorates potential DCS before it kicks in.

6) **Whenever possible, don't "reply-all." Or at the very least, look carefully at the "to" field before sending to avoid reply-all mishaps.** Nathan Zeldes, the president of the Information Overload Research Group, believes that technology solutions are needed to help ease the stress related to reply-all conundrums. In Zeldes's book *Solutions to Information Overload: The Definitive Guide*, he outlines a number of ways companies can lessen the burden of reply-all nightmares. "A number of companies—the Nielsen company for example—have deployed the simplest and most effective solution: remove the Reply All button from the email program's interface. This is usually very easy to do (by an IT group) and has been shown to reduce email load significantly." [5]He goes on to explain that Outlook, the Microsoft email platform, offers administrators the ability to restrict reply-all emails, while Google's Gmail allows users to undo sent emails within thirty seconds if they realize a mistake. A rule of thumb is to imagine your boss and colleagues can read every email you write. If you would feel comfortable accidentally sending an email to your boss or a colleague, chances are there is nothing emotionally charged or upsetting in what you've written.

Self-Assessment Tool #7: How Much Is My Work Being Affected by Dyscommunication?

Do you:

1) Dread opening your inbox—knowing how many emails you must respond to on a given day?

2) Barely have time to read emails in their entirety, skim emails, or delete them after just reading the subject line?

3) Plan to respond to emails but forget to do so?

4) Feel compelled to immediately respond? Feel stressed and anxious when you don't? Or when someone doesn't email you back?

5) Catastrophize and create elaborate narratives about why someone is not getting back to you?

6) Feel that you're being held back in the workplace or aren't as productive because of all the time you spend on digital communications?

7) Respond ambiguously to colleagues or bosses or have trouble interpreting someone's emails or texts?

8) Say things you regret that you would never say in person but feel free to do so through email?

9) Use emails or texts to sabotage fellow employees, or have you yourself been the victim of a sabotage?

10) Act out in a way that causes deep shame or regret, or even jeopardizes your status of employment?

CHAPTER 8

Tactics to Get Your Messages Returned Promptly

Over the course of my long career, I have done several advocacy and fundraising campaigns for various groups and organizations. Since I work daily in this arena—primarily with mass marketing via emails—I can say with some authority what works and what doesn't work when getting people to respond to emails. There is a lot that goes into making these campaigns successful. In fact, I have conducted numerous campaigns, involving millions of emails, and if I had to distill what makes a campaign effective into one essential thing, it is this:

If someone does not open your email, then they are not going to return your email.

Seems obvious, no? So how do we get people to respond to us, so our minds don't go spiraling from broken loops? When talking about how to get people to respond to emails, the answer lies in something as seemingly simple as the subject line. One would think it's easy, but creating a subject line is a subtle and fine art. But its impact is anything but subtle. In fact, the subject line of the email is where all the action happens. It's where a person will gather all the information they need to make the decision to open the email, delay opening the email, or just not open the email at all. Unfortunately, the average person spends the least amount of time thinking about the subject line. However, if you can get the subject line right, you can get people to respond.

So why don't people return our emails in a timely way?

If I haven't made the case clearly enough in the previous seven chapters, I'll repeat it for effect. *It's not about you.* When people don't respond to you, more likely than not it's because *they* are busy or distracted. When an email comes in, their behaviors and thinking go something like this:

- Instead of opening the email, they make a mental note: "I have to get back to Sara."
- But then another email comes in.
- And another.
- "Life" happens all around them.
- Then calls come in.
- People ask them various unrelated questions.
- Texts come in.
- They have their own to-do lists going on in their heads that they were busy executing before Sara's email came in.

- So, they relegate Sara's email in the inbox as something they'll "do later."
- Then, as we are all wont to do, they forget to respond to Sara altogether.

Meanwhile, Sara is back in her office, left with an unreturned message, and her head is spinning. *They hate me. They are doing this on purpose. People suck.* Had they simply opened the email when Sara first sent it and they received it, we would be discussing a vastly different outcome. They wouldn't have forgotten to respond, and they may, in fact, have just responded right away.

Ultimately, what is at play is a short-term memory issue. The research is clear. Short-term memories fade quickly, lasting less than a minute. Some research indicates we are able to hold onto a thought for about eighteen seconds! Don't believe me? Have a person talk to you for thirty seconds or so. Then try to repeat back every single word they said verbatim. It's extremely difficult to do. Our mind can only handle so much at one time. So if we have a running tally while opening emails, such as "Okay, I have to get back to Carol…got to get back to Susan…got to get back to Paul, etc.," we are pushing the limit of what our brains can do. As the short-term memory fades, so do those potential responses to email messages. They simply fade into the inbox, sometimes never to be retrieved.

However, one thing we do know about how the brain and memory work is that the more content someone has the more likely they are to remember. In other words, the more context you give around a memory the better. For example, "I have to email Sara" may be easy to forget. But, if you know that Sara is having an operation and will be out of the office for six weeks and you won't be able to get the report you need from her if you don't respond, you're definitely going to remember the message. So even if you do not respond immediately, you are much more likely to return the message because you have some context in which your memory can respond. The brain now has a lot more information to call on, and the message will not slip into the ether of the short-term-memory void. It's no longer a mere mental note—it's a complete story. In fact, if the story is compelling enough, you may be motivated to respond immediately. That's because, as we noted, our brains are wired to complete the loop.

I know this from my own experience in digital fundraising. Over 80 percent of the donations we receive come from people who open the email and contribute *at the same time.* In other words, the contribution takes place when the email is opened, not later. The same is true of your email. The sooner you get them to open, the sooner you will get your message returned— and the less likely you are to suffer from Dyscommunication.

So, it's not just *if* they open your emails. It's *when* they open the email. *When* matters. A lot. Timing is important. The goal is for them to open the email when they receive it for two important reasons:

1) they are more likely to immediately respond, and
2) the person is less likely to forget and more likely to return the message.

The surest way of having your message returned is to get the person to open your email as soon as possible. They can't read your mind. So just how do we do this? Well, the only piece of information they get before making the decision to open the email are the words in the **subject line.**

Most of us use topical subject lines that reinforce what the message is about. Topical subject lines do little to compel someone to open your email. In fact, topical subject lines decrease the chance of you getting your email returned in a timely way. That's because the person who receives it is quicker to file the email, thinking they know what the email is probably about. "Bill is writing me about the upcoming event. I don't need to read this. I'll look at it later." This topical subject line, along with your name, becomes just another mental note that is easily forgotten.

The best subject lines to get someone to open your email are actually "off-subject" lines. Subject lines that are not predictable will more likely be opened faster. Why? Our brains hate broken loops. If you're at all curious about what the subject line means, you will in fact be motivated to open the email. At first blush, it may seem awkward to use innovative subject lines. *What will the person think? How will they know what the email is about?* The second question is easily answered: They won't know what the email is about if they don't open the email! With respect to the reaction of the recipient, people will read subject lines differently. You need to think about the person you are sending the email to and the context. You can calibrate accordingly. And you can also provide an innocuous segue in the body of the email. For example, say you are going back and forth about some logistics regarding an event. The email exchange is sort of stuck. You send an email with the subject line: "Why China?" *Hmmmm.* Your recipient thinks. *What is this about?* They open the email and then you can simply say: "This has been going on so long, I thought we would move the event to China, then no one will come. :)" It's sarcastic. It's funny. Humor goes a long way, but you'll get a reaction.

At this point, most of us are numb with respect to all the emails we receive. We're exhausted from having to constantly process incoming emails. I find that recipients will understand what you are up to when you try to mix up the subject lines. It's okay to be creative. It can be a lot of fun. You may even brighten people's day. Here are some of the strategies I have used, and all of what I suggest has also been validated by quantitative data.

Ask a Question?

A question requires an answer. When we see a question, we are conditioned to respond. The question should not be something simple like: "Are You Going to the Party?" This is not going to get someone to open the email. The question should be some-what mysterious, which will compel them to open the email, such as "Event Cancelled?"

Funny Subject Lines

Funny subject lines are also effective. A popular one is "We Like Being Used." Another is ***Don't Open This Email ***. So, think of something related to the person you're sending it to and what will make them smile. Another is: "My Bad, Your Fault." "You Struck Out Again," referring to a shared baseball experience. You should also feel free to personalize with inside jokes. Don't be afraid to be provocative.

Single Word Subjects

Another approach is to use just one word in the subject line, but this word should not be topical as we discussed. The word loses its power if it is connected to the email content in an obvious way. A single, unexpected word can raise curiosity and get the person to open the email. A proven winner is "Thanks." *Thanks for what?* That's what I would think and then quickly open the email. Whatever the word being used, it should elicit curiosity. "Truth." Single words without context are mysterious.

Emphatic Subject Lines

This is used even with some regularity, but some words statistically perform better than others. Keywords have been quantified by studies, and some of the data is counterintuitive. For example, "Urgent" has a slightly negative impact on open rates, whereas "bulletin" or "breaking" exponentially impact open rates in a positive way. The key is to use an urgency word that is different from the same old words.

Empty Subject Line

We are so used to emails with subject lines. This is the key part of the problem with topical subject lines. They become rote. Not having any words in the subject line makes the email stand out. It causes curiosity, which can improve open rates. In addition, the person is more likely to read the email carefully to figure it out.

Personal Subject Lines

Using someone's first name in the subject line is sure to catch their attention. However, it loses its effect if it is just an add-on to a topical line. There is little difference between. "Paul, What Day is Good for You?" and "What Day is Good for You?" The first name should be connected to something personal to them. An example, "Paul, Happy Birthday," even if it's not their birthday.

There are many other genres and keywords that work. A simple subject line search will give you thousands of subject lines that you can adapt to your situation. What you need to keep in mind is that an off-subject line is more likely to get them to open your email than a predictable, topical subject line. The whole idea is to raise their curiosity so they will open the email. The sooner someone opens your email, the quicker they will get back to you. If they don't open your email soon after they receive it, it will be placed in short-term memory and all too often forgotten.

Creating Email Content that Elicits a Response

The other half of the battle is the actual content of the email. I have listed a number of ways to improve the clarity and likelihood of having an email responded to in a timely way.

But before you write an email, you must ask yourself what specific outcome you hope to achieve by sending the email.. You need to be clear about what you are asking from them and design the email to elicit this response. You also want to create a limit situation, that is, using words that force a choice. *Yes or No.*

Agree or Disagree. Either/or. It is often the case that the email is hampered from winding narrative before the key point is made. You need to get to the point! People have a lot of emails coming in. You don't want yours to get lost. You need to be specific in what you're asking for. If you use general words like "what do you think," "let me know your feedback," and the like, you're going to get general and ambiguous responses.

You will improve your chances of getting your email responded to if you are clear on what you are asking. You should get to the point quickly. When you get to the point, you should try and force a response using an either/or scenario. Obviously, you will need to soften this to the person and context. As someone who does this for a living, I know a few things that work. Here are some helpful hints to generate emails that get responses:

1. Address the recipient by name.

No-brainer, right? Well, in our rushed and harried world, you'd be amazed how often people miss this important step. Not only is it polite, but it means you know who you're talking to and that the person you are emailing and their time matter. A simple, "Hi Sam!" goes a long way.

2. Start your message with a clear request.

As they say in newspaper publishing, don't bury the *lede*. The lede is news-speak for the most newsworthy part of the story. Don't bog your email down with too much narrative. Get to the point. Start by describing the response you want and what your deadline is. For example, "Please let me know by 11 a.m. what changes you would like made to the blog post."

3. Keep it short.

To boost your response rate by half, keep your email between fifty and 125 words, according to a report by HubSpot, an email-marketing platform. Response rates declined slowly, from 50 percent for 125-word messages to about 44 percent for 500-word messages. After that, it stayed flat until about 2,000 words and declined dramatically.[1]

4. Use a third-grade reading level.

In the same study from Boomerang, cited in the HubSpot article mentioned above, the reading grade level of your emails has a dramatic impact on response rates. Emails written at a third-grade reading level with simpler words and fewer words per sentence were considered optimal, providing a 36 percent better performance rate over emails written at a college reading level and a 17 percent higher response rate than emails written at a high school reading level.[2] Additionally, the study states that free-flowing, informal emails are the best for eliciting responses. (If you want to check your readability level, you can use a website such as ReadabilityScore.com. Drop your message in the text box on their site and see how it rates.)

5. Use the right amount of emotion.

The Boomerang study also found that using a moderate amount of positive or negative emotion words—such as great, wonderful, delighted, pleased, bad, hate, furious, and terrible—increased an email's response rate by 10 to 15 percent over emails that were neutral or strongly emotional.[3] Name-calling, swearing, or making harsh accusations aren't likely to be responded to. In fact, people may outright delete the message and even feel they have cause to ghost you. In other words: You'll never get a response.

6. Use bold font or colors for emphasis.

If you're trying to make a point, use bold fonts and bright colors to highlight the response you'd like to get. Or even add bullet points so the recipient can clearly read what you're asking. Just be sure not to bold the entire email or send it in all caps, because it can come across as **I AM YELLING AT YOU TO DO SOMETHING!** Get my point? It's a turnoff and usually backfires, whereas trying to make a point by using a bold font sparingly for emphasis stands out to the reader.

7. Send your emails out early.

In a *Fast Company* article, "9 Surprisingly Simple Ways to Get People to Respond to Your Email," they cite a study conducted by email tracking software provider Yesware that found out emails sent between 6 a.m. and 7 a.m. get the highest open rates at about 45 percent. The good news is that fewer emails are sent during these time slots, lowering competition.[4] So if you want a response, get up early!

8. Use peer pressure in your favor.

In marketing, peer pressure can be a valuable tool. Like it or not, we tend to respond faster to emails sent to multiple people or those that mention someone in the message. CC'ing a boss or colleague can be seen as tattling, but if you want people to respond, or you need to get something done immediately, it helps to have someone else in on the conversation to hold the recipient accountable to someone besides you.

9. Use the recipient's name as often as possible.

According to a study published by the researchers Dennis Carmody and Michael Lewis, hearing our own name activates parts of the brain connected to self-awareness and self-judgment. [5]In other words, it makes us feel super special and validated as a human being. We are more likely to respond and stay engaged if we see our name—not just in the greeting but throughout the body of the email.

10. Don't be afraid to use humor and compliments.

Just as we love hearing our names being said, we love hearing how wonderful we are too. As Bette Midler once famously said, "But enough about me. Let's talk about you. What do you think of me?" I am not recommending that you compliment others disingenuously. Most people have a built-in bullshit meter.

However, if someone is being thanked or acknowledged for their work, and it rings true, they will more than likely feel the need to respond to you and reciprocate. As far as humor goes, it can be a minefield. Jokes and sarcasm don't always translate well. However, using a light tone or using self-deprecating humor can defuse any tension and help establish rapport. Using various emojis also helps with clarifying emotions and humor in the written form. This can also lighten the mood. If you're embarrassed about something, a simple face-palm emoji helps show that. If you made a joke or are being sarcastic, a winking emoji helps establish that it is indeed a joke—just in case it is not 100 percent clear in the text. If you say something outrageous for hyperbole or effect, a shocked emoji might be appropriate. Overall, if you manage to put a smile on that person's face, they will be much more likely to answer your email and they will be less likely to relegate your email to a to-do list. In fact, they'll be happy to give priority to the next email you send, because they will in fact be looking forward to it rather than dreading it. Who doesn't look forward to hearing compliments?

11. Be aware of attachments.

Often, we must include an attachment with our email. The minute someone sees an attachment, the email is likely to be relegated to the inbox and possibly lost. If people are reading email on their phones, it takes a lot of work to open and get a clear picture. One problem is that people send a lot of useless attachments. Only send an attachment when necessary. If you want a visual image, you can use a screen shot of a key element of the document. If you must send an attachment, and it is not to be edited, then send a PDF, not a Word file. For most email clients, the PDF will show up in the body of the email without having to be opened.

12. When applicable, use technology.

In addition to subject lines and content creation, there is another tool in your proverbial arsenal—technology. There are loads of digital communication tools available to help you follow up and schedule emails. For example, Boomerang offers plug-in tools that let you schedule emails—especially if you're not one to wake up early and send out those important emails. Google's Gmail has also introduced its own version of the feature. Gmail Suite also now has a reminder feature—so if you don't reply within a couple of days, Gmail will move the message back to the top of your inbox.

By following these tips, you should be able to increase the chances of getting people to reply to you more often and prevent Dyscommunication from happening in the first place—at least when it comes to emails. Texts are a different animal altogether.

How to Handle Texting to Help Prevent Dyscommunication

Texts by their very nature imply a conversation is happening. The expectation is when we're texting, we're in the midst of an immediate feedback loop. Many of us think of text as a written phone call. *I say something, then you say something.* It goes on and on until we hang up the phone. However, when texting, these rules don't necessarily apply. There is no formal "Okay, I better be going! Bye!" that happens when most of us text. Nor is there even a guarantee a person is there to "answer" the initial text. Instead, texting is just one massive broken loop. We send out a message and sometimes have no idea if a person has received it, read it, or what they are doing. Then our brains do what they're going to do and start to spin out, desperately trying to complete the loop. So rather than focus on prevention or preemption, I am going to give you practical tactics for text management and best practices to help reduce misunderstandings—like the ones we saw take place in the stories in the previous chapters of this book. Below are several tactics to help mitigate or ward off symptoms before they start.

1. **Remember if you didn't get a reply:** *It's not about you.*
   We have already established that most people are incredibly busy and are receiving hundreds of texts a day. If they're not busy, they just may not feel up to texting or communicating. It's important to remember that texting can feel like an intrusion. We wouldn't just walk into someone's living room and start talking without an invitation, yet that is what texting can feel like to some people. They may be doing something else. They may be driving! They may be out on a walk or in a yoga class. Who knows! No one owes you an immediate response. People have jobs, families, lives. Don't take their lack of response personally.

2. **Don't keep texting if you don't get a reply.**

    Okay, stalker. Step away from the phone. Sending multiple follow-up texts and question marks isn't going to get you a faster response. It's going to get the person you're talking to annoyed. Knowing what we know about how our brain works, the more texts you send and don't get responses to, the more broken loops you're creating. You're setting yourself up to spin out. (Don't worry, in the following chapter, I'll give tactics and tips to help mitigate this if it's already happened.)

3. **Do your part to help set the rules of engagement and a good example—and always respond.**

    Unless the person is in fact a stalker, who you are in no way expected to respond to, do your best to try to respond to someone's text in a kind and reasonably timed manner. If you can't respond right away and want to, but don't have the time or bandwidth, but don't want the other person to worry—simply say: *I'll get back to you later...I'm at work, with the kids, etc.* Again, it reinforces it's not about the sender.

4. **Use Auto-Response technology.**

    There are times that you should never text, and one of those times is while driving. There are a number of auto-response tools and apps now available so that when you're driving and someone texts, they will receive a text back that says, "I'm driving with Do Not Disturb While Driving turned on. I'll see your message when I get where I'm going." Others can be calibrated to say, "I'm not receiving notifications. If this is urgent, reply 'urgent' to send a notification through with your original message."

5. **Be considerate of others' time and schedules.**

Not everyone gets up at 4 a.m. or is up as late as 2 a.m. Unless you know the recipient intimately and know their sleeping schedule, it's best to stick to regular communicating hours. If you want a response from someone, don't send a text when most people are sleeping (typically between 11 p.m.-7 a.m.) unless you know otherwise. If you know your friend or family member is working, it's best to text after working hours.

6. **Keep it short, simple, and to the point.**

As we have already established, people have no time. Keep your texts short and to the point. And like the rules of engagement for emails—get to the point sooner rather than later. Ask a question that provokes a response, such as "Will you be home at five for dinner?" This is more likely to get a response—or even a thumbs-up emoji at the very least. Texting is not the place to be passive-aggressive. "Sure would be nice if you're home by five" will most likely not get a thumbs-up or even a reply. Keep it short and direct and as clear as possible.

7. **Slow down. Write clearly and double-check your autocorrect features.**

I know we're all in a rush, so we've become very lax in our texting, but misspellings, wrong word choices, short or ambiguous phrases, and writing unclearly can lead to all sorts of unnecessary drama. Seemingly small or innocuous comments can become big deals. Slow down and make sure you're saying what you want to say.

8. **Check who you're sending your text to.**

Check who you're sending your messages to. Often texts can be coming in from multiple people at the same time. The last thing you want to do is send the wrong text to the wrong person.

9. **Respond appropriately.**

If someone texts you and asks you a question, and you know it's going to take you more than thirty seconds to reply, then ask to call to discuss or do your best to keep your response as short as the text that came in. Conversely, if someone pours their heart out to you and you respond with a thumbs-up emoji, you can bet you're creating DCS in the sender. Or if you've sent a long, emotional text, and a person replies with "k" (not even the full "okay"), it may be a sign to move on—not only are they not interested in you—they can't even be bothered to text more than a single letter.

10. **Texting is not the place to solve your life's problems.**

A basic rule of thumb is if you don't feel comfortable talking about a subject in person, then it's probably not advisable to discuss over text. I would go so far as to say don't use text messaging to argue or even bring up old personal traumas and problems. If you're trying to defuse a potentially "nuclear" situation, it's best to follow in the footsteps of Robert Kennedy and just go and meet with or talk to the person to resolve the issue.

11. **Use the proper texting laughter/emojis to express feelings.**

There are a lot of ways to get this wrong. You must know what you're doing. For example, saying "Ha" doesn't mean you're laughing. It means you don't find it funny. It's a dismissal. Conversely, HAHAHAHA in all caps conveys that you're actually laughing. (Though it's advisable not to write in all caps because, just as in emails, it comes across as yelling, but some rules are made to be broken.) Emojis can be used to help add a degree of playfulness and to illustrate your responses and feelings. Face palms, shocked face, sweating (anxious) face, silly face, thumbs-up, thumbs-down, hearts, and rainbows all illustrate some sort of feeling that words alone can't always convey. Of course, there are now bitmojis (with expressions on faces that look like you) and memes (i.e., Kris Jenner dancing on a yacht in a leopard print bathing suit or Michael Scott from *The Office* screaming "No! God No!") that help illustrate feelings and convey a tone and playfulness. Use wisely—and sparingly. If you're trying to make a serious point, I would avoid using emojis—even if it's an angry-face emoji. No matter what you do, it will come off as silly, and you will lose the sense of severity.

CHAPTER 9

Solutions for an Unreturned Message

Even when you take steps to cut down on the opportunities for DCS to happen in your own life, unless you throw your cellphone away and close all your email accounts, it's still going to sneak up on you—just hopefully with less regularity. What can you do about it? DCS remedies fall into two categories: the chase (getting the unreturned email or text returned) and in-the-moment remedies.

▌ The Chase

Part of the pain of DCS is feeling like you don't have control— you have emailed or texted a friend, and they didn't text you back, so you just have to wait, and waiting as we know is painful! But it is perfectly appropriate to follow up with people, if you know how to do it artfully (so that you don't become a stalker).

The first remedy to prevent DCS is what I call *the chase*. It's straightforward. We have diagnosed the problem. Most people are inundated with emails and texts and *forget* to respond. The antidote then is also simple: they need to *remember*. Since they have forgotten or are busy, then we are the ones responsible for reminding them. However, for some reason people feel uncomfortable about "following up." They feel nervous and unsure about it. *Will the person think I am annoying? Do I look desperate?* Again, this is just our brain going into worst-case-scenario mode. The reality is most people don't think those things. In fact, they appreciate the reminder.

Emails

I have found a few methods that work surprisingly well when chasing down that unreturned email:

1. **Wait two days.** (If the response required isn't urgent, of course.)
2. **Use an appropriate subject-line strategy from Chapter 8**—to elicit a response (i.e., Event Cancelled, Thank you, Happy Birthday, or ***Don't Open This Email***, etc.)
3. **Whatever you do, DON'T FORWARD the previous email**. This will make a big deal out of the fact that the recipient hasn't returned the first email. It puts the recipient on the defensive, and they'll feel less likely to respond. (Definitely don't send a "Per my last email" note attached to a forwarded email! It's passive-aggressive and won't elicit any meaningful response. In fact, you

may even create a whole new set of problems and added drama.) If you're going to reference the last email, do so obliquely. The new follow-up email should be even more concise than your first email and include a summary of the content you sent previously. I find the best way to approach a follow-up is to act as if the previous email didn't exist at all. Get to the point and ask the question you need an answer to. Often you will get a response back and an apology—or "Thank you so much for the reminder! I've been swamped!"

But what happens if they still don't answer? My best advice is to use a different medium—a text or a phone call. Again, don't make a big deal about the unreturned email. Instead, keep your focus on the question and the response you need.

Texts

Texts, as we know, are different animals altogether. There are basically two different types of text conversations—the first is when you are asking specific questions and need a response to them, and the second is an open-ended conversation that has no specific end. (These latter ones are the ones that wreak havoc on our minds and create the most dysfunction. But they are also the ones that we're dealing with most often—especially in dating and long-term relationships.) So how do we get people to return our texts?

1. **Wait a day.** Again, if it's not something you need an immediate response to, waiting even a couple of days is

appropriate. Then follow up using the tips I recommend below.

2. **Give more context.** As we know, our short-term memories are terrible. The way text messages come in don't help—we either just see a name or a number. Then, as more and more come in, a name and number can slip off the bottom of your screen, never to be seen again. So, there is nothing that can trigger a response. The best way to remedy this is to follow up so you appear again on their screen and to flesh out the text itself with some sort of context, being as specific as possible. For example, if you were on a date with a person, use an inside joke or a reference from the night you spent together. "God, I'm still thinking about that eggplant parmigiana. I can't wait to go back. Didn't you just love it?" The key here is to design the text so you get a response. Be as clear and specific as you can when crafting your question to get the answer.

3. **Go off-topic.** If they don't respond to a specific mention of something, then try going off-topic. (Just as an off-subject line in emails works to elicit responses, so too do off-topic texts.) "Did you see the finale of *Game of Thrones* last night? Crazy right?" The subtext of this is you don't *really* want to know if they watched a television show, you want some validation—your brain is seeking to close an open loop. You want to feel validated and know that the recipient sees "you" (or your texts, rather). Or you can just ask a question outright that

SOLUTIONS FOR AN UNRETURNED MESSAGE

requires a response: "What are you doing for lunch tomorrow? Would you like to go with me?"

What to Do When the Chase Doesn't Work

You've done everything right. You've waited patiently. You've carefully designed subject lines, crafted pointed questions, and you still haven't received a response! Now what? Most likely, your mind is doing what it's supposed to—it is frantically searching to complete the broken loops, and you're beginning to spiral. How do you stop this? What can you do to feel better? Here are two key ways to find instant relief.

In-the-Moment Remedies: Natural Tranquilizers

Thanks to the broken loops, you're spiraling. No matter what you do you can't get out of your own head. With each thought, your advanced mind keeps ramping up. It's telling itself stories now, so catastrophizing is in full swing. Within minutes, you're also having physical responses as well. Perhaps your girlfriend hasn't responded in hours. It's not like her. Now your heart is racing. You may feel short of breath. Your muscles get tense. You just can't settle in your own skin. You have an urge to lash out, maybe text or email her to tell her how upset she's making you. In other words: *You're totally freaking out.*

What you need now is instant relief. You need an in-the-moment panacea that can immediately mitigate your symptoms, a tranquilizer if you will. The reality is we know what causes this problem—the neocortex. Our thinking brain wants to tell itself a story, a worst-case scenario, to close the broken loop. As Albert Einstein wisely stated, "We cannot solve our problems with the same thinking we used when we created them." In this case, our "thinking mind" is what is causing the problems! Therefore, it can't be relied on to fix them. We can't talk ourselves out of it. We can't even talk ourselves down in the moment of it. We need a fast solution that can bring immediate relief—and the quickest way to do so is by activating the parasympathetic nervous system.

The parasympathetic nervous system is part of the brain, but it's not the neocortex. Rather it's made up of the cranial and sacral spinal nerves. The parasympathetic nervous system is responsible for the body's "rest and digestion response." It helps us relax, rest, fall asleep, and digest food. It is the opposite of the sympathetic nervous system that is activated during stressful situations, which raises our heart rate and keeps us awake and alert. Ultimately, the parasympathetic nervous system decreases respiration (our breathing rate) and heart rate and increases digestion fluids and responses. You know your parasympathetic system is working when your pupils are constricted, your heart rate slows, and your blood pressure lowers. In other words—you feel relaxed and at ease. While there are dozens upon dozens of pursuits that have shown to reduce stress hormones and stimulate the parasympathetic nervous system, including singing, meditating, spending time in the woods, going barefoot outside, hot yoga, and acupuncture, some of these things you can't do while sitting in an office waiting on an email or while driving in the car. What you need is an instant parasympathetic response. There are a few body postures and breathing techniques that can help bring immediate relief when DCS gets the better of you.

▌ Body Postures

Though impossible to do while driving, body postures are something you can do while in your office or at home. According to the article "Get Grounded Anywhere: 7 Ways from Teacher Saul David Raye" in *Yoga Journal,* there are several body postures (or *asanas*) that can help activate the parasympathetic response.[1] They are surprising simple. Here are just a few that anyone, in any physical condition, can do:

1) **Earth-Facing Pose**

If you're in a place where you can lie down on the floor, a grounding exercise that has been proven to relax the body is called the Earth-Facing Pose. All you must do is lie face down on your stomach, turn your head to one side, and stretch your arms forward with your palms facing down. Then you breathe deeply into your lower back, filling up your belly slowly with air and exhaling slowing through your mouth. Do this for several breaths. Be sure to monitor where you are holding tension—in your arms, shoulders, neck—and release the contractions in those muscles until you feel relaxed.

2) **Stress-Less Standing Swing**

Stand with your feet hip-distance apart. Raise your arms in what is called the "cactus pose," which looks exactly as it sounds. Raise your arms and bend at the elbows, so your hands point up to the sky and you look like a cactus. Then twist your upper body at the waist, inhaling as you turn to the left, and exhaling as you turn to the right.

3) **Put your legs up the wall.**

Most of us can't do handstands or get upside down. But simply lying on your back with your arms outstretched and putting your legs vertically up against a wall activates the parasympathetic nervous system. Breathe in and out, watching your stomach rise with each inhale and contract with each exhale. Sit like this for about four minutes—unless it's too uncomfortable. You should begin to feel relaxed immediately.

Breathing Exercises

1) **Dr. Andrew Weil's 4-7-8 Breath (The Natural Tranquilizer for the Nervous System)**

Dr. Andrew Weil is a clinical professor of internal medicine and the founder and director of the Program in Integrative Medicine (PIM) at the University of Arizona in Tucson. Weil received both his medical degree and his undergraduate AB degree in biology (botany) from Harvard University and is the author of several books and articles on healthy living. For years he has taught the 4-7-8 breathing technique, which he says can help with reducing anxiety, helping a person get to sleep, managing cravings, and controlling or reducing anger responses. I've found it helps in reducing DCS as well. Here is how it works:

- Before starting the breathing pattern, get into a comfortable sitting position or lie down. Be sure to place the tip of the tongue on the tissue right behind the top front teeth.
- Empty the lungs of air (exhale).

- Breathe in quietly through the nose for 4 seconds.
- Hold the breath for a count of 7 seconds.
- Exhale forcefully through the mouth, pursing the lips and making a "whoosh" sound, for 8 seconds.
- Repeat the cycle up to 4 times.

Dr. Weil recommends using the technique at least twice a day to start seeing the benefits sooner. You can also use it whenever you begin to feel anxiety rising while waiting for a response from an email or text. Dr. Weil suggests, however, not to use this method for more than four breath cycles in a row until you have more practice with the technique; you may become so relaxed you become lightheaded. Therefore, as mentioned above, it is advisable to try this technique when sitting or lying down to prevent dizziness or falls and to not do this one while you're driving.[2] This exercise provides fast results and considerably relaxes your mind and body.

2) **Box Breathing—The Navy SEAL 4x4 Breathing Technique**

Mark Divine, a U.S. Navy SEAL, is a combat veteran who has been called to "relax" in some of life's most stressful and frightening life-or-death situations. Can you imagine having to be calm and not jump to a worst-case scenario before leaping out of a helicopter and into the unknown conditions of a war zone? In Divine's book *Kokoro Yoga: Maximize Your Human Potential and Develop the Spirit of a Warrior*, he advocates the Box Breathing (4x4) Technique that he learned as a Navy SEAL. Like Weil's method, it helps activate his parasympathetic nervous system during highly stressful situations, but not so much so that it renders one drowsy or so relaxed they can't effectively work. If it's a strong enough antidote for SEALs, it is certainly a method to employ when anxious about unreturned messages. Here is how it works:

- Expel the air from your lungs
- Keep the lungs empty for 4 seconds
- Inhale through your nose for 4 seconds
- Hold for a 4 count (don't clamp down or create pressure; be easy)
- Exhale for a 4 count
- Repeat for 10-20 minutes.[3]

This one is also the easiest to remember; just think: *4 x 4. Hold for four, inhale for four, hold for four, exhale for four.*

3) Nadi Shodhana Pranayama or Alternate Nostril Breathing

Nadi Shodhana, also known as Alternate Nostril Breathing, is a powerful ancient breathing practice with wide-reaching benefits. *Nadi* is a Sanskrit word meaning "channel" or "flow," and *Shodhana* means "purification." It's used in yoga to relax and "purify" the body. Among its many benefits—infusing the body with oxygen, releasing toxins, balancing hormones, alleviating allergies, fostering mental clarity, concentration, and alertness— is that it instantly reduces feelings of anxiety. I use this myself in yoga classes, and according to the yoga experts at *Yoga Journal*, here's how it works:

- Choose a comfortable sitting position. Allow the spine to lengthen so that the back, neck, and head are erect throughout the practice.

- Begin by taking one full, deep inhalation followed by a slow, gentle exhalation.

- Then fold the tips of the index and middle fingers inward until they touch the palm at the base of the right thumb. You will alternately use the right thumb to close the right nostril and the right ring and pinky fingers (together) to close the left nostril.

- Use the right thumb to close the right nostril. Exhale gently, but fully, through the left nostril. Keeping the right nostril closed, inhale through the left nostril and fill the stomach with air. As you inhale, allow the breath to travel upward along the left side of the body.

- Next, use the ring and pinky fingers of the right hand to gently close the left nostril and simultaneously release the right nostril. Exhale through the right nostril, releasing the breath down the right side of the body. Pause gently at the bottom of the exhalation.

- Keeping the left nostril closed, inhale once again through the right nostril, allowing the breath to travel up the right side of the body.

- Then again, use the right thumb to close the right nostril as you release the left nostril. Exhale through the left nostril, releasing the breath back down the left side of the body. Pause gently at the bottom of the exhalation.

This completes one round. Repeat the same pattern for each additional round: inhale through the left nostril, exhale through the right nostril, inhale through the right nostril, exhale through the left nostril.

The key to Nadi Shodhana Pranayama breathing is to keep the breath slow, gentle, fluid, and relaxed throughout the practice. You can feel the benefits within as little as five minutes, but you can practice for longer if needed.[4]

In summary, your breath is one of your best defenses against DCS getting out of control. Once you learn the art of expert inhaling and exhaling, you'll likely start to feel better instantly—with or without the response you're waiting for.

CHAPTER 10

It's Not Your Fault

The heart of this book is to help you to deal with problems caused by modern modes of digital communication, but the brain of the book is understanding why *our* brains spin out in the first place. In truth, we can't deal with the stress unless we understand *why* it's happening in the first place. What I hope to have achieved here is to help you understand the process of how Dyscommunication manifests (unreturned and ambiguous messages), the crises that these moments of Dyscommunication create, the syndrome that manifests in us as a result, and what you can do to prevent it or ease the symptoms once it has started. Finally, I have provided you with tactics to ensure that your messages are returned and advice on what to do when they are not.

What's Wrong with Me?

For years, we've believed there must be something wrong with us or we must be crazy when we feel insane or unhinged while waiting on a response from someone. But we're off the hook. It's not our fault. We now know our brains are doing exactly what they should do. They are scanning for solutions, looking for closure, filling the void with stories that the broken loops have left for us. Thanks to digital communication, our minds are full of broken loops. Every inbox we have is full of them—and perhaps there are more than a few of us who haven't responded to our fair share of texts and emails either.

The reality is the broken loops of unreturned messages are not the only broken loops in our lives. The cycle of worst-case scenarios, catastrophizing, and negative loops of thinking show up in other parts of our lives as well.

"Why do we tell ourselves negative stories?" We know the answer now. Our brain needs something final and resolute. And what's more final or resolute than a negative or worst-case scenario? Over the years, we've learned various theories of why we tend to think negatively. We are all familiar with the concept of fight or flight. The idea here is that human beings are innately fearful. This goes back to primitive society when we were extremely vulnerable. Though society may have changed since then, the primitive or reptilian part of our brain is programmed to first turn to fear in an effort to self-protect. Then there is the belief that we are genetically predisposed. Some of us are just by nature worriers. Environment is also a factor. We develop our thinking patterns from the messages we receive from society and/or the external reinforcement we experience throughout our lifetimes. Then there is the matter of our upbringing. Perhaps your parents nurtured you to seek or expect negative outcomes. Or perhaps you have been conditioned on an unconscious level to accrue negative thoughts. Another prominent theory is that a lack of self-esteem manifests in negative thinking. This is by no means an exhaustive list of reasons why we may be wired to look for worst-case scenarios, catastrophizing, and negative loops of thinking. To be sure, all these frames of reference contribute to understanding why we spiral and think negatively. What we have learned through postmodernism is that multiple lenses can explain the same thing, and it is important not to place too much stock in one frame at the exclusion of others. However, what I hope my book adds to this conversation is that there is something meaningful missing from the dialogue—and that is Dyscommunication caused by broken loops.

But You Can Change It

We have already established that our mind is a pattern-creating, narrative-making machine. If we can't complete a pattern, as in the case of an unreturned message, we need to try to complete the pattern by creating a story of our own. But an unreturned call is not the only uncertain and incomplete story in our lives. Most of us have experienced DCS when someone is unusually late. What is important to note is that we do this irrespective of how we were brought up and no matter what messages we have internalized from our environment or experience. We can become worried or anxious if a pattern is broken or incomplete. You can have positive self-esteem, be totally confident, self-actualized, and raised by the world's most caring, compassionate, and loving parents in the world, and still go to a worst-case scenario and think: "There was an accident. My best friend is dead." We do this automatically. It's not because there is something wrong with us. It's not because we're crazy. It's because we have experienced a broken loop, and our mind is doing what it's supposed to—it is telling itself a story to complete a pattern. And then our body responds in kind—we feel anxious, agitated, we begin to catastrophize, take things personally, are unable to talk ourselves down, and then we do or say things we regret and feel ashamed. Just like with unreturned messages, we know there will be a happy ending to the story. The call will eventually be returned, and the person will arrive safely. It's almost always a happy ending. Even so, we put ourselves through hell. Obviously, this is not a cognitive decision we make. If it was cognitive, we would be able to rely on past experiences and know the call will be returned and the person will arrive safely.

There are numerous instances in our life that can kick off a negative loop of thinking. If we are unsure of what the story is due to uncertainty or ambiguity, we will invariably experience a similar situation to that of an unreturned message.

The bottom line is an undiscovered source of our negative loops of thinking is, like the Cuban missiles once were, hiding in plain sight. *It's Dyscommunication.* The brain is just doing its thing. Worst-case scenarios, catastrophizing, and negative loops of thinking are facts of life. Our fearfulness often is caused by the same process as cognition, completing a pattern. Because life is often unpredictable and uncertain, most of us will turn to several worst-case scenarios throughout our days. Since we can't talk ourselves down, we need to seek alternative responses. Instead of berating ourselves, calling ourselves crazy, or feeling inadequate, we can instead understand why we feel the way we do, recognize the pattern (our brain will thank us for that), and then react accordingly—first by setting up emails and texts in a way that elicits responses, and then by following up. And when that doesn't work, we know how important it is to step away from our phones, get physical, and just *breathe*.

ENDNOTES

Introduction

[1] Patrick Kiger, "Key Moments in the Cuban Missile Crisis," History.com, A&E Television Networks, LLC, June 17, 2019, https://www.history.com/news/cuban-missile-crisis-timeline-jfk-khrushchev.

[2] Ibid.

[3] Ibid.

[4] Ibid.

[5] Cable, Ambassador Dobrynin to the Soviet Foreign Ministry Meeting with Robert Kennedy, Wilson Center Digital Archive, accessed May 19, 2020, https://digitalarchive.wilsoncenter.org/document/116955.

[6] "Hotline established between Washington and Moscow," History.com, A&E Television Networks, LLC, November 16, 2009, https://www.history.com/this-day-in-history/hotline-established-between-washington-and-moscow.

[7] Ibid.

Chapter 2

[1] "5 Things You Should Know About Stress," National Institute of Mental Health, accessed May 6, 2020, https://www.nimh.nih.gov/health/publications/stress/index.shtml.

2   David Padgett and Ronald Glaser, "How Stress Influences the Immune Response," *Trends in Immunology,* Vol. 24, no. 8, August 2003: 444-448. doi:10.1016/S1471-4906(03)00173-X.

3   Yun-Zi Liu, Yun-Zia Wang, and Chun-Lei Jiang, "Inflammation: The Common Pathway of Stress-Related Diseases," *Frontiers in Human Neuroscience,* Vol. 11, June 2017: 316. doi:10.3389/fnhum.2017.00316.

4   Eun Joo Kim, Blake Pellman, and Jeansok J. Kim, "Stress Effects on the Hippocampus: A Critical Review," *Learning & Memory,* Vol. *22,* no. 9, September 2015: 411–416. doi: 10.1101/lm.037291.114.

5   Yoichi Chida and Andrew Steptoe, "Response to Mental Stress, Arterial Stiffness, Central Pressures, and Cardiovascular Risk," *Hypertension,* Vol. 56, no. 3, September 2010:e29 doi: 10.1161/HYPERTENSIONAHA.110.156679.

6   Petra H. Wirtz and Roland von Känel, "Psychological Stress, Inflammation, and Coronary Heart Disease," *Current Cardiology Reports,* Vol. 19, September 2017: 111. doi: 10.1007/s11886-017-0919-x.

7   Juliana Menasce Horowitz and Nikki Graf, "Most U.S. Teens See Anxiety and Depression as a Major Problem Among Their Peers," Pew Research Center, February 20, 2018, http://www.pewsocialtrends.org/2019/02/20/most-u-s-teens-see-anxiety-and-depression-as-a-major-problem-among-their-peers/.

8   Gregory Plemmons, Matthew Hall, Stephanie Doupnik, James Gay, Charlotte Brown, Whitney Browning, Robert Casey, Katherine Freundlich, David P. Johnson, Carrie Lind, Kris Rehm, Susan Thomas, Derek Williams, "Hospitalization for Suicide Ideation or Attempt: 2008-2015," *Pediatrics,* Vol. 141, no. 6, June 2018: e20172426. doi: 10.1542/peds.2017-2426.

9   S. O'dea, "Number of Mobile Cellular Subscriptions in the United States Since 2000," Statista, accessed April 25, 2019, https://www.statista.com/statistics/186122/number-of-mobile-cellular-subscriptions-in-the-united-states-since-2000/..

10 "Majority of Americans Say They Are Anxious About Health; Millennials Are More Anxious than Baby Boomers," American Psychiatric Association, May 22, 2017, https://www.psychiatry.org/newsroom/news-releases/majority-of-americans-say-they-are-anxious-about-health-millennials-are-more-anxious-than-baby-boomers.

11 "Americans Say They Are More Anxious Than a Year Ago," American Psychiatric Association, May 7, 2018, https://www.psychiatry.org/newsroom/news-releases/americans-say-they-are-more-anxious-than-a-year-ago-baby-boomers-report-greatest-increase-in-anxiety.

12 "New Figures Workers Reporting Anxiety and Depression Have Risen by Nearly a Third in the Last Four Years," UK Council for Psychotherapy, October 10, 2017, https://www.psychotherapy.org.uk/news/new-figures-workers-reporting-anxiety-depression-risen-nearly-third-last-four-years/.

Chapter 3

1   Phone interview, May 10, 2019.

2   Ibid.

3   Catherine M. Pittman and Elizabeth M. Karle, *Rewire Your Anxious Brain,* (New Harbinger Publications, Oakland, California, Kindle Edition): 1-2.

4   Pittman, 2.

5   Pittman, 20.

6   Pittman, 20.

7   Pittman, 21.

[8]   Pittman, 21.

[9]   Pittman, 21.

[10] Pittman, 51.

[11] Pittman, 51.

[12] Pittman, 52.

[13] Pittman, 52-53.

[14] Pittman, 52-53.

[15] Pittman, 53.

[16] Pittman, 53.

[17] Pittman, 54.

[18] Pittman, 54.

[19] Ray Kurzweil, *How to Create a Mind: The Secret of Human Thought Revealed*, (Viking, New York, New York 2012): 31.

[20] Phone interview, May 10, 2019.

[21] Ryan Holiday and Stephen Hanselman, *The Daily Stoic: 366 Meditations on Wisdom, Perseverance, and the Art of Living*, (Portfolio Penguin, New York, New York 2016): 149.

Chapter 4

[1]   Kross E, Berman MG, Mischel W, Smith EE, Wager TD, "Social rejection shares somatosensory representations with physical pain," *Proceedings of the National Academy of Sciences of the United States of America,* 2011: 108(15):6270–6275. doi:10.1073/pnas.1102693108.

[2]   Durso GR, Luttrell A, Way BM, "Over-the-Counter Relief from Pains and Pleasures Alike: Acetaminophen Blunts Evaluation Sensitivity to Both Negative and Positive Stimuli," *Psychological Science,* 2015: 26(6):750–758. doi:10.1177/0956797615570366.

[3]   DeWall, C. N., MacDonald, G., Webster, G. D., Masten, C. L., Baumeister, R. F., Powell, C., ... Eisenberger, N. I., "Acetaminophen Reduces Social Pain: Behavioral and Neural

Evidence," *Psychological Science,* 21(7), 2010: 931–937. doi: 10.1177/0956797610374741.

4   "POF Survey Reveals 80% of Millennials Have Been Ghosted!" The Latest Catch, *Plenty of Fish,* March 29, 2016, https://blog. pof.com/2016/03/pof-survey-reveals-80-millennials-ghosted/.

5   Peter Moore, "Poll Results: Ghosting," YouGov.com, October 28, 2014, https://today.yougov.com/topics/lifestyle/ articles-reports/2014/10/28/poll-results-ghosting.

6   Beth Lewis, "The Ghosting Guide: An Inside Look at Why Job Seekers Disappear," Indeed.com, August 26, 2019, http:// blog.indeed.com/2019/08/26/ghosting-guide/.

7   Valeriya Safronova, "Exes Explain Ghosting, the Ultimate Silent Treatment," *New York Times,* June 26, 2015, https://www. nytimes.com/2015/06/26/fashion/exes-explain-ghosting-the-ultimate-silent-treatment.html?_r=0.

8   Freedman, G., Powell, D. N., Le, B., & Williams, K. D, "Ghosting and destiny: Implicit theories of relationships predict beliefs about ghosting," 2019, *Journal of Social and Personal Relationships,* 36(3):905–924. doi: 10.1177/0265407517748791.

Chapter 5

1   Pittman, 52-53.

2   Pittman, 52-53.

3   Pittman, 52-53.

4   Radesky J, Miller AL, Rosenblum KL, Appugliese D, Kaciroti N, Lumeng JC, "Maternal mobile device use during a structured parent-child interaction task," *Academic Pediatrics,* 2014, Vol. 15, no. 2: 238-44. doi: 10.1016/j.acap.2014.10.001.

5   Influence Central, *Kids & Tech: The Evolution of Today's Digital Natives,* 2016.

6   Craig Timberg, "Many teens sleep with their phones, survey finds—just like their parents," *Washington Post,* May 29, 2019, https://www.washingtonpost.com/business/technology/mimicking-their-parents-many-teens-sleep-with-their-phones-survey-finds/2019/05/28/1bf2ee68-8188-11e9-9a67-a687ca99fb3d_story.html.

7   Sean Grover, L.C.S.W., "The Best Technology-Screen Time Contract for Kids," *Psychology Today,* April 19, 2018, https://www.psychologytoday.com/us/blog/when-kids-call-the-shots/201804/the-best-technology-screen-time-contract-kids.

8   Lori Cluff Schade, Jonathan Sandberg, Roy Bean, Dean Busby & Sarah Coyne, "Using Technology to Connect in Romantic Relationships: Effects on Attachment, Relationship Satisfaction, and Stability in Emerging Adults," *Journal of Couple & Relationship Therapy,* 12:4, 314-338. doi: 10.1080/15332691.2013.836051.

9   McDaniel, B. T., & Coyne, S. M, "'Technoference': The interference of technology in couple relationships and implications for women's personal and relational well-being," *Psychology of Popular Media Culture,* 2014. doi: 10.1037/ppm0000065.

Chapter 6

1   Andrea Clariss Hernandez, "28 Texting and Driving Statistics Every Driver Should Know," https://policyadvice.net/car-insurance/insights/texting-and-driving-statistics/#cell-phone-use-while-driving-statistics.

2   Ibid.

3   Ibid.

4   Ibid.

5   Ibid.

6   Ibid.

7   Ibid.

8   "Facts and Statistics for Texting and Driving," *PersonalInjurySanDiego.org,* 2019, https://www.personalinjurysandiego.org/topics/facts-about-texting-driving/.

Chapter 7

1   Caitlin Dewey, "How many hours of your life have you wasted on work email? Try our depressing calculator," *Washington Post,* October 3, 2016, https://www.washingtonpost.com/news/the-intersect/wp/2016/10/03/how-many-hours-of-your-life-have-you-wasted-on-work-email-try-our-depressing-calculator/?utm_term=.96b32760cfbb.

2   Kruger J and Epley N, "Egocentrism over email: Can We Communicate as Well as We Think?" *Journal of Personality and Social Psychology,* 2005, Vol. 89, No. 5: 925-936. https://faculty.chicagobooth.edu/nicholas.epley/krugeretal05.pdf.

3   Angela Lashbrook, "Why Reply All Emails Are Always the Wrong Move," *Forge,* December 17, 2018, https://forge.medium.com/why-reply-all-emails-are-always-the-wrong-move-82e4388e369b.

4   Mike Rosewald, "Eradicating 'Reply All,'" *Bloomberg,* November 21, 2012, https://www.bloomberg.com/news/articles/2012-11-21/eradicating-reply-all .

5   Lashbrook.

Chapter 8

1   Mike Renahan, "Ideal Length Sales Email, Based on 40 Million Emails," *Hubspot,* https://blog.hubspot.com/sales/ideal-length-sales-email.

2   Ibid.

3   Alex Moore, "7 Tips for Getting More Responses to Emails," *Boomerang,* https://blog.boomerangapp.com/2016/02/7-tips-for-getting-more-responses-to-your-emails-with-data/.

4   Stephanie Vozza, "Surprisingly Simple Ways to Get People to Respond to You," *Fast Company,* March 30, 2016, https://www.fastcompany.com/3058316/9-surprisingly-simple-ways-to-get-people-to-respond-to-you.

5   Dennis P. Carmody and Michael Lewis, "Brain Activation When Hearing One's Own and Other's Names," NCBI.com, https://www.ncbi.nlm.nih.gov/pmc/articles/PMC1647299/.

Chapter 9

1   *YJ* Editors, "Get Grounded Anywhere: 7 Ways from Teacher Saul David Raye," *Yoga Journal,* April 12, 2017, https://www.yogajournal.com/poses/get-grounded-tap-parasympathetic-nervous-system-anywhere.

2   "How to use 4-7-8 breathing for anxiety," *MedicalNewsToday,* https://www.medicalnewstoday.com/articles/324417#how-to-do-it.

3   Reuben Brody, "Here, Have a Secret Breathing Technique from a Navy SEAL," *InsideHook,* May 6, 2016, https://www.insidehook.com/article/advice/secret-navy-seal-breathing-technique-box-breathing.

4   *YJ* Editors, "Channel-Cleaning Breath," *Yoga Journal,* April 12, 2017, https://www.yogajournal.com/poses/channel-cleaning-breath.

ACKNOWLEDGMENTS

I'd like to extend my gratitude to the following people. Terri Bishop. Terri is a friend and a thought partner. She edited the initial outline and introduction of the book which significantly impacted its trajectory. Jamie Paisley for her feedback and suggestions. She is a lifestyle coach and has hands on experience with the issues discussed. The late Dr. John Sperling for his inspiration, wisdom, and erudition. My mother, Marty, who was a reliable sounding board and provided helpful suggestions. My partner Bei who supported my writing. Half of the book was written during the COVID lockdown. She provided me a warm habitat and supported me with love. I would like to thank James Miller and Ken Aronson for their exceptional work in the preparation of the book. My gratitude to all of my teachers.

ACKNOWLEDGMENTS

ABOUT THE AUTHOR

 Sam George is a master at two things: discerning trends before they are recognized as trends and communicating these ideas to the public at large. He is the co-author of *The Great Divide: Retro vs. Metro America* (Polipoint Press, 2004), the first book to name and bring awareness of the cultural rift in America, which has become a war. *The Great Divide* received national press coverage, including reviews in the *New York Times, Newsweek,* the *Los Angeles Times,* and a presentation to National Press Club that was covered by C-SPAN.

In 1995, Sam was hired to put together a strategy to legalize marijuana. The program was in part funded by George Soros. Sam's focus groups and polls showed that the only way to "legalize" marijuana was to "medicalize" it first. Another funder, John Sperling, Founder of University of Phoenix, described it as a "genius" idea. It worked. A total of thirty-three states have approved medical marijuana, and ten states have legalized marijuana.

Sam now splits his time between writing and digital communication. He specializes in advocacy, marketing, and fundraising for nonprofits and corporations. He also leads an entirely online yoga company, YMEDICA, which educates yoga teachers on medical yoga.